Dominique François

82nd Airborne Division
1917-2005

HEIMDAL

Editions Heimdal - Château de Damigny - BP 61350 - 14406 BAYEUX Cedex - Tél. : 02.31.51.68.68 - Fax : 02.31.51.68.60 - e-mail : Editions.Heimdal@wanadoo.fr

Dominique François

Translated by Trevor Jones

82nd Airborne Division
1917-2005

This book is dedicated to my grandfather, Joseph François, a cavalry officer during the Great War, killed on June 6, 1944 at Saint-Marcouf, whose sons Joseph, Jules and Fernand (my father) were liberated by the paratroopers of the 82nd Airborne Division...

...and to the paratroopers of the "All American" Division.

Introduction

The 82nd Airborne Division has seen some of the American Army's most elite soldiers pass through its ranks, men such as Sergeant Alvin C. York and General James M. Gavin. But the 82nd does not owe its reputation to these men alone. The history of this glorious Division has been forged by thousands of anonymous paratroopers, always prepared to jump in extreme situations and accomplish their objective on the ground, whatever the conditions.

From the trenches of the Somme to the Iraqi Desert, from the Normandy bocage to the snow-covered forests of the Belgian Ardennes or the Vietnam jungle, the paratroopers of the 82nd Airborne Division have accomplished their missions, never failing to do their duty.

They earned their spurs on the battlefields of Saint-Mihiel, La Fière, Groesbeek, Hue and more recently Basra.

The men with their jump wings pinned proudly to their chests wear on their shoulders the famous "AA" patch of the "All American", the distinctive sign of the 82nd Airborne Division.

They have been the spearhead of the American Army for almost 90 years.

It was therefore important to pay tribute to these men by retracing the history of the Division through this Memorial album which includes nearly one thousand photographs, virtually all published for the first time, from private collections and the Division's archives.

It took me over ten years to archive these photographs, meet these veterans in France and in the United States and collect their anecdotes.

Sadly, some of them are no longer with us to read this book published today. Without them, nothing would have been possible.

I hope that this Memorial Album will find its place on the bookshelves of both those interested in military history and of the young generations taking over from their forebears.

Acknowledgements

The author would like to extend his thanks to the following people:

Marty Morgan (historian at the D-Day Museum, New Orleans); Colonel Frank Naughton; General Paul Smith; Colonel Erik Peterson, military attaché at the American embassy, at OB. Hill; Lieutenant-Colonel Chester Graham; Z. Frank Hanner (director of the National Infantry Museum at Fort Benning); Jack Williams (son of Lt. Gen. Williams); the family of Colonel Louis Mendez; Colonel Roy Creek; Marcus Heim (DSC); George Leidenheimer; Captain Chris Heisler; Mrs. Skip Mac Grath; Captain Robert Rae (DSC) and his son-in-law Albert Parker; Jack Schlegel; and everyone else who contributed to this book; my children, already interested in the History of these men, and my wife, who supported me throughout this extensive and lengthy project, for her wise advice and the translation work.

« *Where is the prince who can afford so to cover his country with troops for its defense, as that 10,000 men descending from the clouds might not, in many places, do an infinite deal of mischief before a force could be brought together to repel them.* »
Benjamin Franklin, 1784

« …Un prince qui pourrait s'offrir une armée pouvant couvrir son pays, composée de dix mille hommes, descendant des nuages, en plusieurs endroits, pourrait causer d'infinis dommages avant qu'une force ne puisse se regrouper pour les repousser… »
Benjamin Franklin, 1784

Table of contents

1

First World War

American officers in a barracks in the United States. (Ph. NA/D. François.)

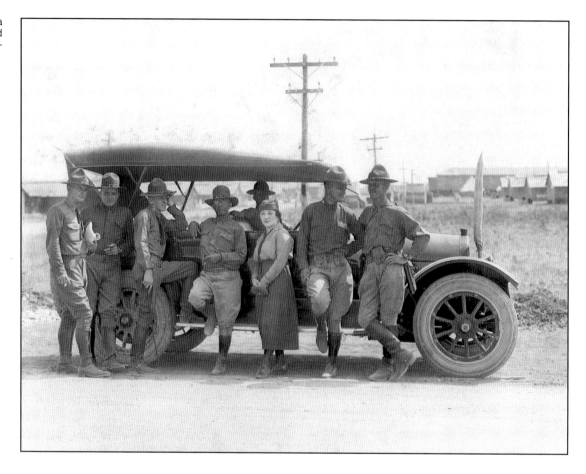

America enters the war

In 1914, when the First World War broke out in Europe, the United States Army comprised only 63,870 men of whom some 45,000 were stationed overseas. The regular army was backed up by nearly 27,000 troops in the National Guard, who could be mobilized in case of emergency. Faced with the increasing risk of a growing conflict, in December 1914 General Leonard Wood helped to form the National Security League. Wood and his organization called for conscription as a means of increasing the size of the US Army. President Woodrow Wilson responded by increasing the standing army to 140,000 men.

When the USA declared war on Germany in April 1917, Wilson sent the American Expeditionary Force (AEF) under the command of General John Pershing to the Western Front.

The Selective Service Act was quickly passed by Congress, authorizing President Woodrow Wilson to raise a volunteer infantry force of not more than four divisions.

In September the draft was passed: all males between the ages of 21 and 30 were required to register for military service. By September 12, 1918, 23,908,566 men had registered. Around 4 million men were immediately sent into the armed services. Of these, 50 % served overseas during the war.

By July 1918 there were over a million US soldiers in France.

The American Expeditionary Force suffered 264,000 casualties during the war, with a death toll of 112,432.

A new division is created

The History of the "All-American" Division started at the beginning of the century, while the First World War had been ravaging Europe and the Mediterranean basin since 1914. The United States managed to remain neutral until 1917, but various incidents ended this neutrality.

The 82nd Infantry Division of the National Army was formed on August 25, 1917 at Camp Gordon at Georgia near Atlanta, with men from Alabama, Georgia and Tennessee. By November 1917, approximately 28,000 men were barracked at Camp Gordon. The 82nd Infantry Division was born, in a period of war, austerity and shortages.

The 82nd Infantry Division was organized into two infantry brigades of two infantry regiments each and an artillery brigade containing three artillery regiments. The division was supported by an engineering regiment, three machine-gun battalions and a transportation company composed of munitions transport and a medical and sanitary corps.

Until it entered the war, the United States army was anything but ready. The transformation of recently drafted civilians into soldiers was carried out under very hasty conditions. For most of them, there was a severe shortage of rifles, webbing equipment and suitable quarters as well as, in many cases, uniforms. The sections, companies and battalions were drilled with wooden rifles.

After a few weeks, the division received a consignment of 1917 Eddystone rifles. Webbing equipment started to appear progressively. The division then took part in basic shooting training on the Waycross firing range. During the first three months of 1918, the "All-Americans" received training on offensive techniques and trench warfare, supervised by a group of Franco-British officers.

Training on the use of special weapons was unfortunately just theoretical. Although the division had an automatic weapon firing school, with a dozen French Chauchat machine guns, there were none at regimental level. Colt machine guns were used by machine gun companies although they were never delivered to the front.

During the months of February and March 1918, the War Department wrote favorable reports on the progress of the training of the 82nd Division. The reports concluded that the division had received sufficient training to be sent overseas. The 82nd Division was the second division from the National Army (in other words not from the regular army or troops of the National Guard) to be sent to France and the eighth American infantry division to go overseas. In April 1918, the Regiment received orders to leave Camp Gordon and move to Camp Upton, New York.

The 82nd arrives in Europe

On April 10, 1918, the "All-Americans" left Georgia and started out to New York. After a short stay, the division set sail for England on the 25th and the first soldiers arrived on May 7. Between May 7 and 17, the unit made a few stopovers in various camps in England before leaving Southampton for Le Havre. Before being transferred to France, however, the 325th Infantry Regiment was chosen to parade in London before the King of England and a large crowd. This parade of the 325th was a historical event, since it gave the British people a glimpse of the brand new American army.

The general staff of the Division reached the front at Escarbotin in the Somme, France, on May 16, 1918. During their short stay in Le Havre, the soldiers exchanged their US model 1917 rifles for British rifles and were issued British helmets and gas masks.

The division then occupied the towns and villages west of Abbeville, over a vast sector. The troops immediately started a training program under the supervision of the 66th British Division. The unit was issued Lewis LMGs, Vickers machine guns and Stokes mortars. For transport, the English used horses which were supplied to all battalions in the division. Training was intensive, with an English unit briefing the new arrivals in bayonet fighting and life in the trenches. The Americans

quickly assimilated these new techniques and became specialists in using the Lee-Enfield rifle and the Vickers machine gun.

Early in June 1918, the division sent small groups of officers and NCOs to the front, in the British held sector of Amiens and Albert. It was during one of these visits that Captain Jewett Williams of the 326th Glider Infantry Regiment was killed on June 9. He became the first 82nd soldier to give his life in combat.

The British and American forces had agreed that the American battalions would serve under the orders of the British army. This decision was cancelled, however, by an order transferring the division to the Toul sector. All British weapons had to be returned and the 1917 model rifles reissued. On June 16, the division changed sector, taking two days to reach Toul.

The towns and villages north of Toul were occupied by the division and, once again, training exer-

1. Soldiers of the 320th Machine Gun Battalion training at Camp Gordon, Georgia. They are using a Lewis light machine gun. (Ph. NA/D. François.)

2. On April 25, 1918, the "All-American" set sail from the quays of New York for England. (Ph. NA/D. François.)

cises, designed to familiarize the soldiers with their new weapons, resumed. The infantry were issued French Chauchat light machine guns and the machine gun companies were equipped with Hotchkiss 8 mm heavy machine guns. By then, all units of the division apart from the 159th field artillery brigade had returned to the headquarters. In the meantime, the artillery continued to train at La Courtine, in northern France.

First contact with the enemy

The 82nd, sent to relieve the 26th Infantry Division, had to occupy a section of the Woevre front known as the Lagny sector.

One battalion from each of the four infantry regiments had to occupy the front line and the outposts. One battalion from each regiment had to stay behind in support, whilst the 3rd battalion of the regiment was held in reserve. The comman-

ders of the selected battalions, with their company commanders, had to go on reconnaissance missions, to familiarize themselves with the land where the fighting would soon take place.

The first units of the division sent into action were the 2/325th IR (commanded by Major Hawkins), the 1/326th IR (Major Wells), the 3/327th IR (Major Hill) and the 2/328th IR (Major Buxton). The relief of the 26th ID by the 82nd started during the night of June 25, 1918. The machine gun companies joined up with the infantry battalions on the front line on July 5, artillery support being provided by French artillery units.

During the days and night spent in the Lagny sector, the division quickly gained considerable military experience and discovered what life in the trenches was really like. Offensive patrols were carried out and the division not only retained control of No man's land but also penetrated deep into enemy positions on numerous occasions. Several of these incursions, with no artillery support, led to violent clashes with the enemy. Numerous soldiers were injured or killed in these skirmishes, especially during exfiltrations.

On August 4, 1918, companies K and M of the 326th Infantry carried out a raid with artillery support against a German position, opposite the positions held by the regiment. The officers and men had been well trained for this operation by French officers on a similar position built behind the front. The raid was executed with exceptional skill, penetrating 600 meters into enemy territory and destroying an enemy patrol. The American captured three machine guns, numerous rifles, pistols and other weapons. Only one American was killed and four injured during this raid.

When all the soldiers had managed to return to their trenches, the German artillery, supposed to have been knocked out by preparatory fire, started a barrage of fire causing numerous American casualties. A total of 17 men were killed and 15 others injured by shellfire.

Marbache sector and Saint Mihiel offensive

After two months spent in the Lagny sector, the 82nd was considered as experienced and therefore as an independent division. The men had discovered the harsh reality of trench warfare. They would have to learn even more. The division was ordered to maneuver towards the Marbache sector to relieve the 2nd Infantry Division on the front line. The relief started on August 15, 1918 and was completed in two days. The Marbache sector, located along the valley of the river Meuse, includes the town of Pont-à-Mousson. Until the arrival of the 82nd Division, it was reputed to be a peaceful sector. The enemy had become more aggressive in the sky, artillery fire was efficient and there were numerous reconnaissance patrols.

The 157th Field Artillery Brigade joined the division shortly afterwards and received a warm welcome by the infantry units, which quickly appreciated the benefit of having artillery support. The officers of the 157th had developed close relations at Camp Gordon with the cadres of the 82nd, which created a link between the two units.

The first major American offensive of the war was launched on September 12, 1918. It was known as the St Mihiel Offensive. The objective of the operation was to reduce a large enemy pocket of enemy resistance jutting into the allied lines. The American forces engaged in the operation acted like the two pincers of a giant claw moving together. The 82nd was assigned to a position on the right flank of the force located on the left shoulder. The first elements of the division gave the assault at 0500 hours.

The enemy resistance expected failed to materialize. The German battalion occupying the village of Norroy, one of the main objectives as the division advanced, had abandoned the village. It had retreated so quickly that it had left behind the battalion archives and a considerable amount of equipment. The liberated villagers gave the soldiers a fantastic welcome.

It was during this offensive that lieutenant-colonel Emory J. Pike, Division machine gun officer, became the first of the "All-Americans" to be awarded the Congressional Medal of Honor. During the assault on the town of Vandières by elements of the 328th Infantry Regiment, LTC Pike went forward to reconnoiter new machine gun positions. Heavy artillery shelling had disorganized the advance of the infantry units. Putting his own life in danger, LTC Pike reorganized his men and covered their position. When one of the men in the outpost was wounded, he immediately went to his rescue. While administering first aid, Pike was fatally wounded when another shell burst in the same place. LTC Pike was one of the 78 officers and privates killed in action during this operation.

On September 24, the 82nd received orders to move to the Clermont region, west of Verdun. The horses and artillery were transported before the division. The 82nd reached its new sector on September 25 and pitched camp in the woods west of the road running between Clermont and Bar-Le-Duc. Divisional headquarters were set up in a farmhouse at Grange-Le-Comte. At this time, the division was composed of 934 officers, 25,797 privates and 5,646 animals.

On September 26 at 0100 hours, the 82nd was woken up by the sound of massive artillery fire. It was the intensive preparatory barrage, the prelude to the famous Meuse-Argonne campaign. The division in reserve was now on alert. The 82nd Division had to be ready to move out in two hours.

Three days later, the situation seemed to worsen in the Apremont sector, the men of the 327th Infantry were sent into the sector with two ammunition belts and two days rations. The 327th had to advance without its machine guns, and without its auto transportation company and its supply company. The regiment was already en route after taking less than one and a half hours to break

Depot of American trucks in Brest, before they left for the front. (Ph. NA/D. François.)

1. General Pershing awarding the Distinguished Service Cross to Major General C.D. Rhodes, when his division was attached to the 82nd, at Beau Désert in the Gironde, June 3, 1919.

2. An officer of the division presenting a ribbon to a horse during a ceremony at Prauthoy, December 14, 1919.

3. Cavalrymen of the 82nd during a ceremony at Prauthoy in the Haute Marne, December 14, 1919.

4. Major General Geo Duncan, division commander, presents a ribbon to the flag of the 307th Field Signal Battalion, 82nd Division, for its bravery in action.

(Photos NA/D. François.)

camp. In view of this performance, the next day Brigadier General Craig, Commander-in-Chief of the 1st Corps, made the following comment: "The 327th Infantry Regiment reached its objective last night in a remarkable time in spite of major difficulties".

The soldiers of the 327th were positioned in a sector where they had to protect a vulnerable area of the front. After two days in this position, the regiment was relieved by elements of the 1st Division. Its work accomplished, the regiment was authorized to pull back to Varennes. On October 6, 1918, the 82nd was ordered to replace the 28th Infantry Division on the front and prepare to launch an attack on the German positions the next morning. The attack was launched as planned, by the 164th Brigade of the 82nd Division, including the 327th and 328th Infantry Regiments.

The 164th Brigade successfully secured the assigned objectives, Hills 180 and 223, but was unable to take the town of Cornay due to fierce German resistance. On October 10, the 325th relieved the 327th and 328th and attacked northwards with the 326th. The two regiments cleaned up the sec-

tor including the eastern half of the Argonne Forest and captured the zone south of Saint-Juvin, the river Aire with the town of Cornay.

On October 31, 1918, after 27 days of constant pressure on the enemy forces, the order was sent for the 77th and 88th Divisions to relieve the 82nd Division.

The 82nd Infantry Division suffered heavy losses in the Meuse-Argonne Offensive, with 902 officers and privates killed in action, 185 taken prisoner, 25 missing and 4.897 injured, making a total of 6.009 casualties during 27 days fighting. On November 11, 1918 at 1100 hours, 10 days after the 82nd was relieved, the long-expected order to cease fire was finally given. The war was over.

After an extended stay in the Prauthoy sector, in February 1919 the men of the 82nd Infantry Division were ordered to prepare for the return home. On March 2, the division set off for Bordeaux, traveling for 2 days and 2 nights. On April 20, all units of the division set sail for New York.

At New York, the division was distributed into various transit camps, Camp Upton, Camp Dix and Camp Mills, and demobilized shortly after.

During the war, the 82nd Infantry Division spent a total of 105 days in action, advanced over 10 miles (17 km) on the front and captured 845 German soldiers. The division's casualties were 1,035 killed in action and 6,387 wounded.

For service to the Nation, the soldiers of the "All-American" won two Medals of Honor, three Distinguished Service Medals and 75 Distinguished Service Crosses.

The legend of the "All-American" division was born.

Above: Brigadier General. R. Lindsey, commanding the 164th Infantry Brigade of the 82nd at Beautrian in the Gironde. (Ph. NA/D. François.)

Opposite: the 307th parading after receiving its decoration, during a ceremony in the Gironde. (Ph. NA/D. François.)

Group of men from the division, decorated for their bravery during fighting on the Meuse-Argonne front. (Ph. NA/D. François.)

Command post of the 2nd Battalion in the Argonne Forest. (Ph. NA/D. François.)

Beaumont American cemetery, Sedan sector. (Ph. NA/D. François.)

Soldiers firing a salute during the ceremony at Beaumont. (Ph. NA/D. François.)

American ceremony at Beaumont cemetery on May 30, 1919. (Ph. NA/D. François.)

General Pershing is present at the ceremony. (Ph. NA/D. François.)

Soldiers of the 82nd Infantry Division embarking for Europe. (Ph. NA/D. François.)

Franco-American ceremony at Thiaucourt in the Meurthe-et-Moselle, May 30, 1919. (Ph. NA/D. François.)

The legend of Sergeant York

During the month of October, the Meuse-Argonne Offensive witnessed an extraordinary exploit by a man who was to retain a place of honor in the greatest traditions of the United States Army, Sergeant Alvin C. York.

On October 8, 1918, the 2nd battalion of the 328th Infantry Regiment was confronting the enemy on Hill 223, near the village of Châtel-Chehery. Early in the morning, the battalion's attack was bogged down under mortal fire from enemy machine guns located on a hill to the south west, on the other side of the valley. Company G was ordered to knock out this position. A detachment composed of four NCOs and 13 men was detailed to circle around the back of the hill and silence the machine gun nest.

The 17-man patrol succeeded in advancing 400 meters behind the enemy lines and surprised 75 German soldiers with their major, who was giving instructions for a counter-attack against the Americans. Thinking that this patrol was the spearhead of a large force, the Germans dropped their weapons and started to surrender.

German machine gunners on the hill overlooking the scene, however, quickly took advantage of the situation and opened fire on the Americans, killing and wounding 9 out of the 17 members of the patrol. Corporal Alvin York dived to cover. Using the German prisoners as protection, the corporal, who was a skilled sharpshooter, shot at the enemy soldiers whenever they raised their heads to fire, killing a total of 18 men. Six enemy soldiers continued firing at York.

York then resorted to hunting tricks (before the war, he used to go hunting wild geese in the woods of Tennessee) first shooting at the one farthest away, then the next, emptying the five-round ammunition clip of his M.1917 rifle. He shot his last enemy with his Colt 45, at very close range. York killed 14 others before capturing the German commander. Bewildered by such a display of courage, the German officer blew his whistle and 30 other Germans got up and surrendered. The captured officer then asked Corporal York whether he was English. York simply answered, "I'm American". The corporal ordered his prisoners to form a column, guarded by the 7 remaining able-bodied Americans. A few hours later, York managed to get 132 prisoners back to the lines of the 2nd Battalion.

The Commander-in-Chief of the American Expeditionary Corps in Europe, General John J. Pershing, called York: "the greatest civilian soldier of the war". York was promoted to sergeant and later became the second soldier of the 82nd Infantry Division to be decorated with the Congressional Medal of Honor. The French Marshall Foch, Supreme Commander of the Allied Forces, was to say about York's feat in the Argonne: "what you did was the greatest thing accomplished by any private soldier of all the armies of Europe".

Above: CP of the 2nd Battalion in the Argonne Forest at Marcq in the Ardennes. (Ph. NA/D. François.)

Below: Saint Juvin bridge, crossed by the infantrymen of the 2nd Battalion on October 11, 1918, during violent fighting. (Ph. NA/D. François.)

Above: CP of the 327th to the north of Châtel Chehery, Hill 223. (Ph. NA/D. François.)

Below: men of the 2nd Battalion of the 327th, on Hill 180 about half a mile (1 km) from Fleville in the Ardennes, October 8, 1918. (Ph. NA/D. François.)

1. A village in the Lagny sector where the 327th was engaged in action. Captain Collins was taken prisoner during the fighting here. (Ph. NA/D. François.)

2. Headquarters of the 327th at the Mesnil farm, Châtel Chehery in the Ardennes. (Ph. NA/D. François.)

3. Medical unit of the 327th at Fleville, Châtel Chehery sector. (Ph. NA/D. François.)

4. Command post of the 326th on Hill 223 at Châtel Chehery. (Ph. NA/D. François.)

5. Bridge over the river Aire, south of Saint Juvin, crossed by companies E, G, H on October 11, 1918. (Ph. NA/D. François.)

6. Regimental CP of the 326th at Argonne, October 11, 1918. (Ph. NA/D. François.)

Above: infantrymen of the 82nd next to a gun abandoned by the Germans, Chehery sector in the Argonne Forest. (Ph. NA/D. François.)

Below: Y.M.C.A rest center at Bordeaux. (Ph. NA/D. François.)

Above: mobile medical unit of the 307th Sanitary Train, 82nd Division, March 5, 1919. (Ph. NA/D. François.)

Opposite: entrance of a warehouse, formerly occupied by the Germans. (Ph. NA/D. François.)

Group of American officers at Tonnerre in the Yonne, January 20, 1919, with Major General Walther H. Gordon, commanding the 82nd Division. (Ph. NA/D. François.)

Two mail transport vehicles. (Ph. NA/D. François.)

Above: Chehery castle, in the Ardennes region, occupied by the Germans then by the general staff of the 82nd Infantry Division. (Ph. NA/D. François.)

Below: Co "K" of the 805th Pioneer Infantry in the Meuse. (Ph. NA/D. François.)

General John J. Pershing, Commander-in-Chief of the American Expeditionary Corps in Europe, inspecting the men of the 56th Pioneers. (Ph. NA/D. François.)

Depot of trucks at Dijon. (Ph. NA/D. François.)

Headquarters of the 82nd Division at Prauthoy, January 17, 1919. (Ph. NA/D. François.)

1. Major W.A. Cunningham with a corporal of the 321st Machine Gun Company from the 82nd Division, awarded the DSC for bravery during action in the Argonne Forest, April 19, 1919. (Ph. NA/D. François.)

2. Major W. Cunningham. (Ph. NA/D. François.)

3. German prisoners. (Ph. NA/D. François.)

ning base and the infantry school. His assistant commander was Brigadier General Matthew B. Ridgway.

The 82nd, located at Camp Claiborne in February 1942, was trained by members of the 9th Infantry Division.

On June 26, General Bradley was transferred to take command of the 28th Infantry Division at Camp Livingston.

A new weapon

Due to its heroic past in Europe, on August 15, 1942, the division received the immense honor of becoming the first airborne division in the US Army. The successes of the German airborne troops in

1. General Lee, known as "The Father of the Airborne", at Fort Benning in 1940. He was later to command the 101st Airborne Division. (Ph. Fort Benning/D. François.)

2. The role of the "Test Platoons" was to design the new airborne infantry concept, by preparing the training and the equipment of the new paratroopers. (Ph. NA/D. François.)

3. These paratroopers are wearing "Ridell" football helmets and the first model 1941 jump suits. (Ph. NA/D. François.)

The inter-war period

The 82nd Infantry Division was demobilized on May 27, 1919 at Camps Mills, New York, after returning from the front in Europe.

On June 24, 1921, the division was reconstituted and regained its place in the Army. The Division Headquarters was organized at Columbia, South Carolina in September 23, 1921. The elements of the Division were located in South Carolina, Georgia and Florida.

During this peace-time period, it was not engaged in any major events but acted as one of the echelons in the organization of the Army Reserve forces.

With war once again raging in Europe, Japan's surprise attack on Pearl Harbor brought the United States into war with, as before, an army ill-prepared to cope with such a conflict.

On March 25, 1942, the 82nd Infantry Division was reactivated at Camp Claiborne, a new base outside Alexandria, Louisiana, along the Red River.

Major General Omar N. Bradley was appointed to take command of the division. A graduate from West Point, Bradley commanded the Fort Ben-

Holland, Belgium and Crete clearly demonstrate today the value of this new weapon.

After Bradley, General Ridgway took command of the division, with the ambition of making his division the spearhead of the US Army.

The news was not received with a great deal of enthusiasm by the troops, however. Most of the men had no idea of what this really meant. In 1942, going off to fight in a glider or jumping by parachute was unusual, to say the least, and gave rise to a considerable amount of apprehension and fear.

Training then became more intensive, the men who had not requested their transfer were convinced that they were taking part in a great adventure and that they were members of an elite force, a feeling which was soon to help create the myth of the paratrooper.

The original organization of the new airborne division consisted of one Parachute Infantry Regiment of 2,000 men and two Glider Infantry Regiments of 1,600 men each, as well as artillery and support units.

The 504th Infantry Regiment was selected to become the Parachute Infantry Regiment (PIR) of the 82nd airborne Division and the 325th and 326th Infantry Regiments were to become the future Glider Infantry Regiments (GIR).

The 504th PIR, formed on May 1, 1942, was initially commanded by Colonel Theodore L. Dunn, later to be replaced by his Executive Officer, LTC Reuben H. Tucker.

Every soldier in the division had to qualify as a paratrooper at the Airborne Troops School at Fort Benning, Georgia. During several weeks training, the soldiers had to complete practice jumps from towers of different heights and five jumps from aircraft to obtain their "wings", awarded at the end of the course. Conditions at Fort Benning School were rudimentary. Canvas tents were erected alongside wooden barracks. At the entrance, the motto suggested the spirit of the school: "The toughest paratroopers in the world go under this gate." During this initial physical preparation phase, the instructors, all former drill sergeant in the infantry, put the pressure on every batch of volunteers. Daily reveille at 5 a.m., then 5 miles jogging followed by intensive physical exercise interrupted by classes on the basics of parachuting and parachute packing sessions. Discipline was extremely strict: wherever they went, soldiers always had to run, even when on their own, according to the saying that parachutists never walk. The slightest infringement of the numerous camp rules was immediately sanctioned by the instructor. For jump training, the men dropped first from the 34-foot tower then the 250-foot tower. At the end of the course, each trainee had to complete five jumps from a C-47, including one jump by night.

Fort Bragg

The Division then moved headquarters to a new base, at Fort Bragg, North Carolina. The division was transferred in October 42, and was joined by the 504th PIR, the 376th Parachute Field Artillery Battalion and Company C 307th Airborne Engineer Battalion, all newly formed. Training intensified at Fort Bragg, the paratroopers continued making practice jumps but also took part in tactical exercises involving the problems encountered in the field.

4

5

4. At the dawn of the airborne era, the paratroopers' outfits and equipment had not yet been standardized. (Ph. NA/D. François.)

5. Four towers were built at Fort Benning to train the paratroopers. (Ph. Fort Benning/D. François.)

Page 30 continued

The American Waco CG-4A glider

At the end of the Second World War, the bombers and fighter aircraft could fly at tremendous speeds and engage combat using tactics and firepower far exceeding that of the fragile biplanes that had taken to the skies in the First World War. Tank armor was more and more impenetrable, shells were more and more powerful. The static trench warfare of the First World War had given way to the Blitzkrieg, so brilliantly implemented by the Germans. The footsoldier's equipment had evolved considerably since the Battle of the Somme. The First World War, which had served as a testing ground for weapons and equipment, had led to improvements in the entire military arsenal available in 1940.

Quite unlike all these technical innovations and improvements, however, a new weapon was to appear during the Second World War, which had never been used previously in combat. Especially designed for this conflict and never used again since the end of the War, this weapon, which was to transport thousands of soldiers in silence to every Theater of Operation, carry through the air vehicles which were heavier than itself, this weapon, with its fragile wooden and tube construction, was no other than the glider.

Amongst all the models built by the various countries engaged in the fighting, one was mass produced and used in all Theaters of Operation by the United States Army, the Waco CG-4A.

The construction effort at the start of the conflict to produce the American glider is one of the heroic adventures of the American war industry, an adventure which has remained in the shadows. It all started in February 1941, when General Henry Arnold, Chief of the US Army Air Corps (the US Air Force did not yet exist) ordered a study on the creation of a glider intended for military purposes. By the end of 1946, when all the production chains had shut down, over 16,000 gliders had been built. The cost was phenomenal, even for a major power used to investing huge amounts of money in technical innovations. Over 500 million dollars were spent on the various study and construction programs.

A dozen American companies across the USA took part in a glider design study. Each aviation industry replied to the specifications prepared by the Air Corps, which was then able to examine each project and select those meeting the size, weight and construction criteria.

The Waco Aircraft Company, located at Troy, Ohio, was selected. Founded in 1921, this small company had considerable experience in the production of commercial aircraft. The first design contract was signed in June 1941 for an 8-passenger glider and a 15-passenger glider. In September, Waco submitted a first design report on tests carried out in a wind tunnel. The project was accepted in 1942 and the go-ahead was given to start production immediately. Shortly afterwards, however, the Air Corps realized than an 8-passenger glider could not be used in combat and made a request to change the contract. The 100 gliders which had already been built were reused later for training purposes. The new, larger glider could carry 15 passengers and was named CG-4 then CG-4A.

Upon delivery, the CG-4A was regarded with contempt by the Air Corps pilots who nicknamed it the "boxcar". It is true to say that the CG-4A had nothing in common with the superb aircraft being produced at the time. Although more elegant than its English counterpart the Horsa AS 51, its lines were nevertheless angular.

The Waco was selected for mass production and construction started in numerous companies. The production cost of a CG-4A varied between $15,000 and $25,000, depending on the companies.

The CG-4A was built from more than 70,000 parts. Like the Horsa, the CG-4A was designed for two pilots with dual controls. The first models only had single controls.

The CG-4 and its variant CG-4A were built to transport 15 troops or a jeep and its crew. It could transport a payload greater than its own weight. Built from a fabric-covered tubular steel frame and wooden parts, it was extremely light. Access was via a portside door for personnel, and the entire nose section (including the pilot's compartment) of the glider swung upward to unload larger cargo. The wings, ailerons and floor were made from plywood, the fuselage was covered with doped cotton fabric.

The C-47: the "tug" aircraft

The C-47 aircraft was used to tow the CG-4A, without difficulty, even when the glider was carrying a jeep. The C-47 sometimes even towed two gliders side by side. Tests were also attempted to parachute men from a C-47 towing two gliders, but this technique proved too dangerous to be implemented. The CG-4A was designed to fly at a speed of about 140 mph (220 km/h), which is quite compatible with the speed of a C-47.

The glider pilots communicated with the C-47 cockpit via a telephone wire wrapped around the tow-rope stretching between the tail of the aircraft and the nose of the glider.

A tragic accident...

The Robertson Aircraft Corporation at Saint Louis, Missouri, was one of the companies manufacturing the CG-4A. During a demonstration flight on August 1, 1943, less than eleven months before the D-day landings, 5,000 spectators gathered at Lambert Field for an air show which included a Waco glider. Various officials from the town, including the Mayor, William Dee Becker, were invited on board to appreciate the glider's silent flight.

A C-47 airplane took off, towing the glider from the nose. After an uneventful period of flight, one of the wings suddenly broke off from the glider. The CG-4A plummeted 2,300 feet (700 meters) to earth, killing everyone on board. An inquest was immediately carried out to determine the causes of the disaster. Sabotage was initially suspected but examination of the wreckage was soon to indicate a manufacturing flaw.

In spite of this accident, the CG-4A was used in all theaters of operation from North Africa to Normandy, from Holland to Burma. It even served to drop Chindit Commandos behind the Japanese lines. It was an excellent cargo glider but suffered, apart from its vulnerability, from the fact that it could not carry a jeep together with its trailer or its howitzer. Two gliders were in fact required to transport a 75 mm howitzer, its crew and the jeep to tow it.

The other problem was the number of passengers, since 15 soldiers did not form a unit in the allied forces.

It was abandoned in 1946, and progressively replaced by a new aircraft which made its debut in the Korean War, the helicopter.

The parachute

The parachute is the parachutist's most important item of equipment. An object of apprehension, it must be reliable and efficient. It was to undergo a constant series of improvements, and is now virtually 100 % reliable. In the 1940's however, the parachute was new and far from being risk-free.

The first parachutes adopted by the Test Platoons (test groups whose role was to test the new "airborne weapon" concept) were those used in the Air Force and issued to pilots, modified by the addition of an automatic opening system. The first parachute was the type 4 (T-4), which was quickly replaced by the T-5 manufactured by the company Irvin. Its 8.50 m canopy consisted of 28 panels and had a vent allowing air to escape, to reduce oscillations. From the leading edge to the harness attachment points where they separated into four web risers, the shroud lines were 6.70 m long. The harness straps went over the shoulders and between the legs and were attached together by steel buckles. The parachute was opened by the 5 m long static line, hooked onto a cable in the aircraft with a carabiner. On jumping, the strap uncoiled and tightened under the combined weight of the parachutist and the propeller blast, extracting the canopy then the shroud lines.

Although safe and practical, the T-5 had two non-negligible disadvantages during use: the violence of the opening shock and the amount of time required to remove the harness on landing. In contrast, the British X-Type parachute, in service since 1940, which opened "shrouds first", considerably reduced the opening shock and its quick release fastening allowed the parachutist to take off the harness by simply pressing on it.

The companies Irvin and Switlik had agreed to supply 3750 T-5 parachutes for July 1941, but by October none had been received. The problems were solved and, by the end of July 1942, production had reached 20 000 parachutes a month.

Reserve chutes, fitted on American parachutes since the beginning, were only adopted by the British in 1955. The British argued that the use of a reserve chute demonstrated a lack of trust in the reliability of the main chute, that it was cumbersome and handicapped the jumpers both on the ground and during the drop, and lastly that it incurred unjustified expenses.

Training at Fort Benning. (Ph. Fort Benning/D. François.)

The Glider Regiments discovered their new means of transport, the WACO CG-4A glider, which could carry 15 troops, or a howitzer, a jeep or other vehicles and supplies and equipment.

Due to the difficulties in transporting two infantry regiments by glider, the structure of the division was modified. The 326th Glider Infantry Regiment was replaced by the 505th Parachute Infantry Regiment commanded by General James Gavin. The 456th PFAB (Parachute Field Artillery Battalion) and the 782nd Airborne Ordnance Maintenance Company were also attached to the division.

Two officers joined the newly converted division, Brigadier General Maxwell Taylor, commanding the division's artillery and Brigadier General Keerans who became the division's assistant commander.

In March 1943, the division was reviewed by General Marshall and Sir Anthony Eden, Foreign Minister of Great Britain. The two men considered that these new units foreshadowed the future armies.

On March 29, as commander of the 505th PIR Colonel Gavin took part in the division's first true exercise, by parachuting onto the bridge over Wateree River near Camden, South Carolina. A large number of VIPs, including Winston Churchill and General Marshall, were present. Although a military success, the exercise was saddened by the accidental death of three paratroopers, struck during the jump by an aircraft which had lost engine power.

Having demonstrated the success of this type of operation, the 82nd Airborne Division was informed that it would soon be posted overseas. In April, the division was transferred to Camp Edwards, Massachusetts, then to New York before setting sail for North Africa.

Jump familiarization from a gondola. (Ph. Fort Benning/D. François.)

The Fort Benning towers. (Ph. Fort Benning/D. François.)

Lieutenant Donald Graul, was one of the first to be posted at Fort Benning, before being transferred to the 507th Airborne Regiment. He was taken prisoner in Normandy. (Ph. D. François.)

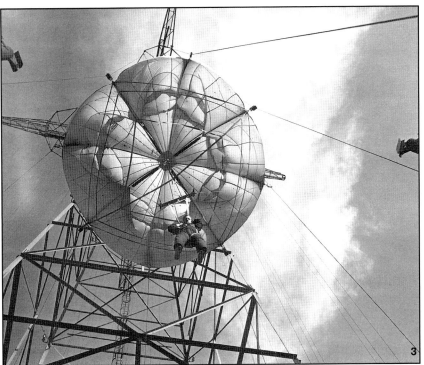

1. Soft landing from the tower. (Ph. D. François.)

2. Equipment / control room of one of the towers. (Ph. Fort Benning/D. François.)

3. Thousands of paratroopers completed their first practice jumps from these 250-foot towers. (Ph. D. François.)

4. Practice jump on the Fort Benning DZ. (Ph. D. François.)

Training equipment at Fort Benning. (Ph. D. François.)

Navigation classes were required to mark out the jump zones. (Ph. D. François.)

1. The first jumps were made from a tower with canopy deployed. (Ph. D. François.)
2. This paratrooper, posing for the photograph, shows the position at the door, even if jumping while holding a rifle is inconceivable. (Ph. D. François.)
3. Two paratrooper generations, father and son. (Ph. NA/D. François.)
4. General Marshall, accompanied by high-ranking officers, visiting the Airborne Troops school. (Ph. NA/D. François.)

1. The last training phase before graduation was a jump from the top of a tower, canopy deployed. (Ph. D. François.)

2. The 34-foot towers were used to train the paratroopers how to jump out of the aircraft and how to land. (Ph. D. François.)

3. Impressive photograph of the four towers at Fort Benning. Two are still in service today. (Ph. D. François.)

A wind machine provided the wind needed to teach the soldiers how to unharness their chutes during landing. (Ph. NA/D. François.)

General Marshall meeting the instructors of the Airborne Troops School at Fort Benning. (Ph. NA/D. François.)

Numerous visitors came to look around Fort Benning. This photograph shows the parachute packing room. (Ph. NA/D. François.)

The paratrooper's special equipment, including the T-5 parachute. (Ph. NA/D. François.)

An instructor showing the soldiers how to unharness their parachutes when the wind is blowing in the canopy. (Ph. D. François.)

Various practice jumps on the Fort Benning DZs. (Ph. D. François.)

A paratrooper with a radio antenna. (Ph. NA/D. François.)

This paratrooper, being helped by his comrades, has just jumped from one of the 250-foot towers. (Ph. D. François.)

Paratrooper being dropped from a tower. (Ph. D. François.)

1. The paratrooper is pulled up with his parachute open to the end of the tower arm, from which he will be released. (Ph. D. François.)

2. This young paratrooper completed his jump with ease, maybe thanks to his good luck charm? (Ph. Fort Benning/D. François.)

3. A sergeant distributing candy to young paratroopers in the train taking them to Fort Bragg. (Ph. Fort Benning/D. François.)

Above: paratroopers in their harnesses learning how to use their web risers. (Ph. D. François.)

Below: from this platform, the soldiers learn the first movements to be carried out when jumping. (Ph. Fort Benning/D. François.)

At Camp Mackall, transport of heavy equipment in a C-47 is taught on training fuselages. (Ph. D. François.)

A few months later, the C-47 was to be regarded as the workhorse of the American Army. (Ph. D. François.)

This photograph shows a jeep which is to be taken on board with its soldiers and the crew of a gun. (Ph. D. François.)

Below: C-47 fuselage for training on loading and stowing heavy equipment. (Ph. D. François.)

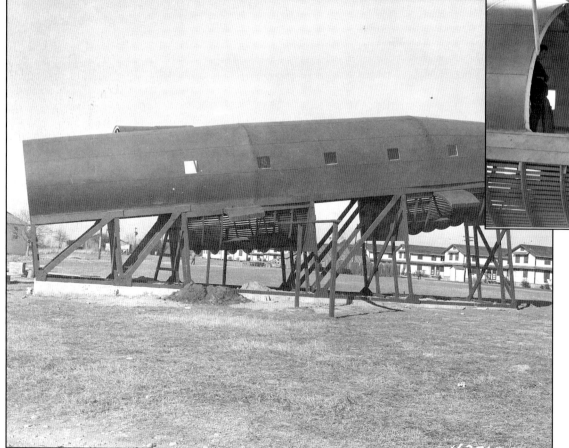

Above: two officers watching a jeep and a howitzer being loaded on a C-47. (Ph. D. François.)

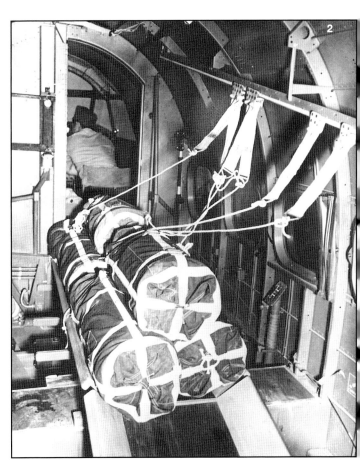

MOCK TOWER
PARACHUTE SCHOOL
FORT BENNING, GA.
1943

1. 34-foot tower. (Ph. D. François.)
2. Drop of A-5 containers. (Ph. D. François.)
3. Practice jump at Camp Mackall. (Ph. D. François.)

1. Practicing the roll on landing. (Ph. D. François.)

2. Paratroopers from the 507th transporting a container. (Ph. D. François.)

3. A paratrooper from the 502nd Parachute Regiment has just been captured by reserve troops during an exercise. (Ph. Fort Benning/D. François.)

4. The jumpmasters equipped with special parachutes waiting for their sticks. (Ph. D. François.)

TROOPERS OF
THE 502d JUST
LANDED IN AIR
ATTACK

The 501st Parachute Battalion, after the Test Platoons, receives the future cadres of the airborne regiments. It would later become a regiment and be attached to the 101st Airborne Division. (Ph. Fort Benning/D. François.)

General Lee reviewing the instructors of the 501st Parachute Battalion. (Ph. Fort Benning/D. François.)

During a ceremony at Columbus, a town close to Fort Benning, General Lee meets the future cadres of the airborne regiments. (Ph. Fort Benning/D. François.)

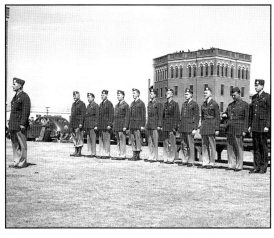

These officers who formed the nucleus of the airborne troops will soon be put in command of a regiment. (Ph. Fort Benning/D. François.)

At Fort Benning, a batch of reserve chutes ready for distribution to the paratroopers who are getting ready in the background. (Ph. D. François.)

Colonel Roy Linquist commanding the 508th PIR, watches his men training at Fort Benning. (Ph. D. François.)

Colonel Linquist and Major Shanley, from the 508th PIR, watch their men during the various training phases. (Ph. D. François.)

Sgt. Carlson Smith from the 507th PIR with the regiment mascot, Geronimo. (Ph. D. François.)

Stick of Medics ready for a drop. (Ph. D. François.)

These three paratroopers are wearing M.1941 jump suits and helmets. (Ph. D. François.)

Two paratroopers from the 508th getting ready to board a C-47 for a practice jump at Camp Mackall. (Ph. D. François.)

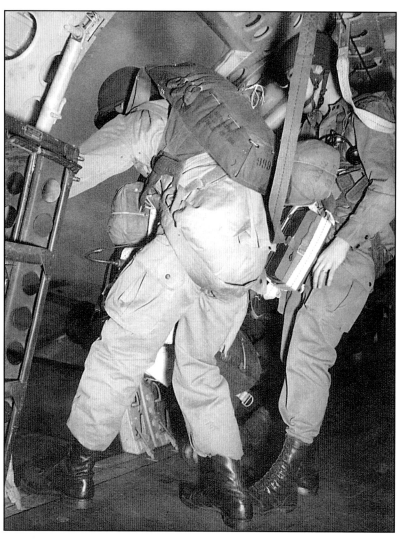

Jump at Camp Mackall. (Ph. D. François.)

At Camp Mackall, paratroopers are equipped for a practice jump. The Griswold bag containing the dismantled M1 Garand rifle is worn under their harness. (Ph. D. François.)

This paratrooper from the 507th, demonstrates a rather unusual way to use a .30 caliber machine gun. (Ph. D. François.)

Behind the Camp Mackall barracks, the paratroopers equipped with a shortened T-handle shovel, a T-5 parachute and an M1 Garand rifle, get ready to make a jump under combat conditions. (Ph. D. François.)

Jump from a C-47. (Ph. D. François.)
Arrival on the drop zone. (Ph. D. François.)

Pvt. Fred Carden was one of the first to join the paratroopers. He was later transferred to the 508th. (Ph. D. François.)

The brand-new paratroopers are proud to pose for the photograph which will then be sent to the family. (Ph. D. François.)

Equipment to use the harnesses at Fort Benning. (Ph. D. François.)

Three paratroopers wearing Ridell helmets. (Ph. NA/D. François.)

A general from the Argentine Army visits Fort Benning. (Ph. NA/D. François.)

Interesting photograph showing a paratrooper from the 507th, armed with an M1-A1 rifle and a .30 caliber machine gun, inside a case for the Garand rifle. (Ph. D. François.)

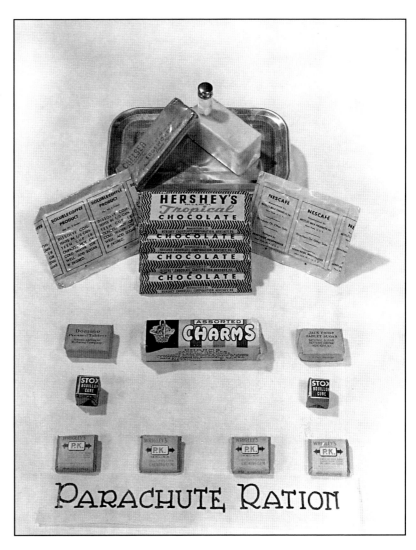

Parachute ration. (Ph. NA/D. François.)

Although serious accidents during training were rare, a parachute did sometimes fail to open. The outcome was often fatal. (Ph. D. François.)

A cameraman has come to film a jump, the paratroopers get into the newspaper headlines. (Ph. D. François.)

Paratroopers jumping from a C-47 at Alliance, Nebraska. (Ph. D. François.)

The C-47 was to carry thousands of paratroopers throughout these war years and even after, during the Indochina war. (Ph. D. François.)

Practice jumps for these men from the 507th. Note the insignias painted on the helmets. (Ph. D. François.)
These two paratroopers are taking part in maneuvers involving several regiments from the 82nd Airborne. (Ph. D. François.)

This paratrooper poses in front of a photographer for a newspaper. (Ph. D. François.)

A paratrooper from the 507th jumping with the stars and stripes at Alliance, Nebraska. (Ph. D. François.)

Ceremony at Camp Mackall. (Ph. D. François.)

Recreation room for paratroopers from the 507th PIR at Alliance, Nebraska. (Ph. Marty Morgan.)

Officials and reporters come to meet these new soldiers, the elite of the US Army. (Ph. Marty Morgan.)

Paratrooper showing his equipment. He is armed with a Thompson machine gun. (Ph. D. François.)

General Gavin and Colonel Lindquist talking during a cocktail at Fort Bragg. (Ph. D. François.)

Exhibition jump at Camp Mackall. (Ph. Marty Morgan.)

1. Paratroopers from the 507th returning from an exercise. (Ph. Marty Morgan.)

2. C-47 cockpit. (Ph. D. François.)

3. General Omar Bradley, who was to command the 82nd for several months before being replaced by General Ridgway. (Ph. NA/D. François.)

Opposite: General Matthew B. Ridgway, who was to command the 82nd Airborne Division. (Ph. NA/D. François.)

Below: a new means of transport emerges during the Second World War: the glider. This photograph shows the American-built Waco CG-4A. (Ph. D. François.)

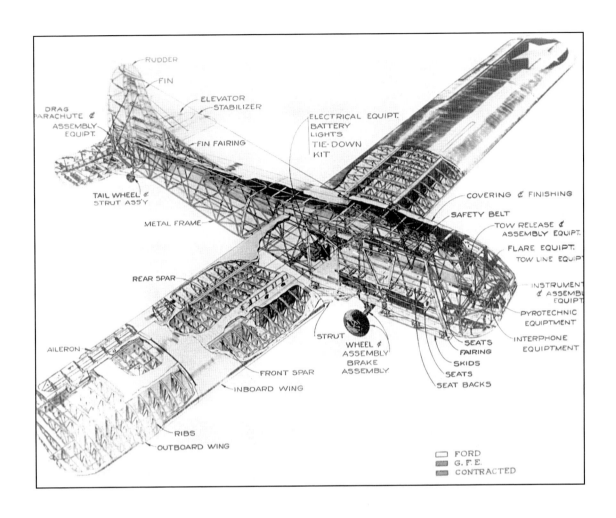

RUDDER
FIN
ELEVATOR
STABILIZER
ELECTRICAL EQUIPT.
BATTERY
LIGHTS
TIE-DOWN
KIT
DRAG
PARACHUTE &
ASSEMBLY
EQUIPT.
FIN FAIRING
COVERING & FINISHING
SAFETY BELT
TOW RELEASE &
ASSEMBLY EQUIPT.
FLARE EQUIPT.
TOW LINE EQUIPT.
TAIL WHEEL &
STRUT ASS'Y
METAL FRAME
INSTRUMENT
& ASSEMBLY
EQUIPT.
PYROTECHNIC
EQUIPTMENT
INTERPHONE
EQUIPTMENT
REAR SPAR
SEATS
FAIRING
AILERON
STRUT
SKIDS
WHEEL &
ASSEMBLY
BRAKE
ASSEMBLY
SEATS
SEAT BACKS
FRONT SPAR
INBOARD WING
RIBS
OUTBOARD WING

□ FORD
▨ G. F. E.
▨ CONTRACTED

73

Captain William Nation of the 508th PIR, here at Camp Blanding in Florida. He was killed in January 1945 in the Ardennes. (Ph. D. François.)

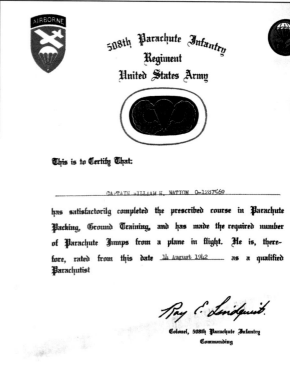

William Nation's parachutist certificate. (Ph. D. François.)

Parachute packing room in 1941. Within a few months specialized units of "Riggers" would be given responsibility for this important job. (Ph. D. François.)

Above: Captain Robert Rae of the 507th, with his men during a practice jump. (Ph. D. François.)

Opposite page: propaganda poster for the airborne troops, encouraging the public to buy war bonds. (NARA.)

they've got the GUTS

GIVE 'EM MORE FIREPOWER

Propaganda posters for the airborne troops, encouraging the public to buy war bonds. (NARA.)

Stick of parachutists. (Ph. D. François.)

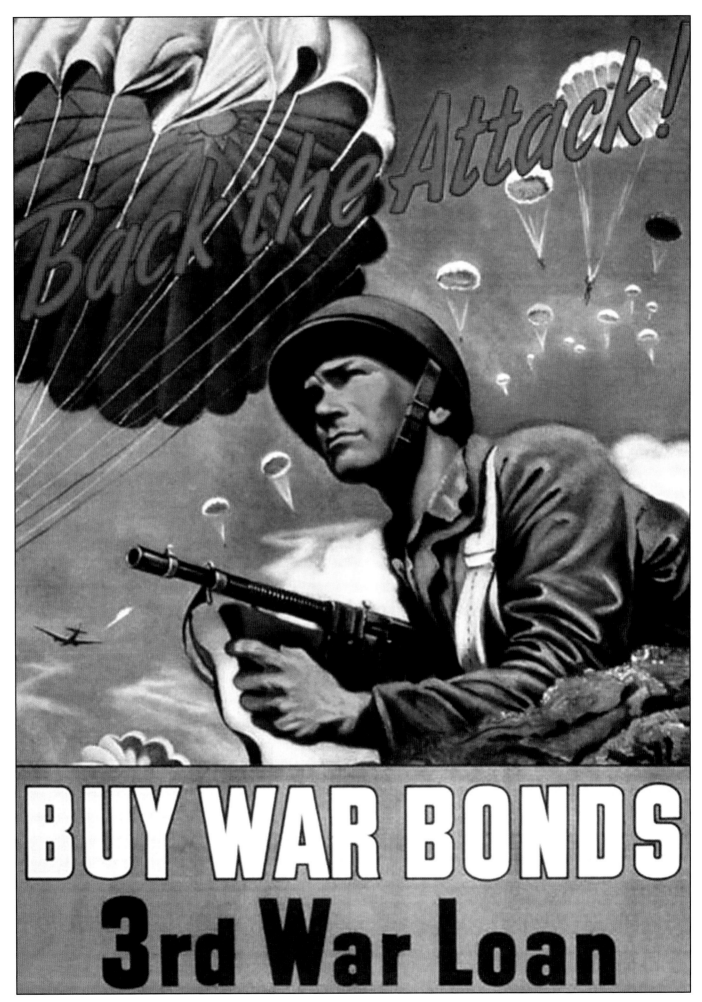

Fort Benning jump tower as it is today. (Ph. D. François.)

Parachutists during jump training. (Ph. D. François.)

Louis Mendez' parachutist certificate. A few months later
he was to command the 3rd Battalion of the 508th PIR.
(Coll. D. François)

Brigadier General Leo Donovan, Commanding the 1st Airborne Brigade, Major General Chapman, Commanding the Airborne Command review Colonel George Millett and Lance Corporal Worne of the 507th PIR. (Ph. D. François.)

Sadly, there was the occasional fatal accident during practice jumps. (Ph. D. François.)

Bivouac camp of the 508th PIR during an exercise. (Ph. D. François.)

Major Gordon Smith of the 507th PIR. A few months later he was to be made a prisoner of war after parachuting in Normandy. (Ph. D. François.)

Captain Robert Rae who in a few months time was to be awarded the DSC for bravery during the Battle of the La Fière bridge in Normandy. (Ph. D. François.)

Parachutists of the 507th PIR during an exercise. (Ph. D. François.)

First model of the Waco glider. (Ph. D. François.)

Lt. Frank Naughton of the 507th PIR, he was to be dropped far from his drop zone, during Operation Neptune and defended the village of Graignes. (Ph. D. François.)

Parachute Group Headquarters

Certificate of Proficiency

This is to Certify That ___Private Francis E. Naughton, 36045078, Co. "A", 504th Parachute Bn.,___
has satisfactorily completed the prescribed course in parachute pack-
ing, ground training, and jumping from a plane in flight. He is,
therefore, entitled to wear the special insignia of the Parachutist and
be rated from this date, _____February 2, 1942_____, as a qualified
Parachutist in the Army of the United States.

R. Chase

18359—Benning, Ga., 5-7-41—2,500

Major, 504th Parachute Battalion.

Frank Naughton's parachutist certificate. (Ph. D. François.)

Soldier from the 505th PIR at the wheel of an experimental model of jeep. (Ph. Marty Morgan.)

Waco CG-4A glider. (Ph. D. François.)

Postcard of Camp Mackall showing airborne artillerymen training. (Coll. D. François.)

Postcard of Camp Mackall. (Coll. D. François.)

Wooden fuselage for the exercises on jumping from the aircraft. (Ph. D. François.)

Pvt. Frank McKee, of the 508th PIR, who was to be gravely injured in Normandy during the battle to take Hill 95. (Ph. D. François.)

The parachutists had to have excellent training in close-combat fighting, to prepare them for the tough time ahead. (Ph. D. François.)

Manual issued at Camp Mackall to the new parachutists of the 82nd Airborne Division. (Ph. D. François.)

1. The song distributed to paras of the 82nd Airborne. (Ph. D. François.)

2. On November 4, 1943, the 508th PIR celebrated its first anniversary. (Coll. D. François.)

3. Manual issued at Camp Mackall to the new parachutists of the 82nd Airborne Division. (Ph. D. François.)

4. Jack Summers and Paul Mank from the intelligence section of the 507th PIR. (Ph. Remy Bouron.)

North Africa

General Ridgway was deeply concerned about this rushed movement, the various units in his division had not had enough time to train together, due to all these reorganizations and movements. But he knew that his men would do their best and adapt to the situation.

After 12 days at sea, the men of the 82nd Airborne reached the port of Casablanca, Morocco.

In November 1942, General Patton's troops had landed in Morocco and started their offensive against the Axis forces in Africa.

During the afternoon of May 10, 1943, the paratroopers from the "All American" hit the African soil. The division set up temporary camp on the heights of the town before boarding train for Oujda, which appeared somewhat "rustic" to men coming from a country where comfort was taken for granted.

Despite the harsh weather conditions, the camp at Oujda attracted numerous visitors and officials from North Africa who wanted to meet this new division, including Lieutenant General Mark Clark, General Spaatz, General Patton and General Bradley and, of course, the Commander-in-Chief of the Allied Forces in North Africa, General Dwight D. Eisenhower.

The division stayed at Oujda for six weeks. Training resumed, while the only thought on everyone's mind was the question where, when and how? Training took place at night, since it was impossible to carry out certain exercises under the scorching sun. Night

Above: Colonel James Gavin parading at Oujda with the 505th PIR. (Ph. 82nd ABN/D. François.)

Below: officers from the 82nd Division discussing the preparations for the Operation to be carried out in a few days time in Sicily. (Ph. 82nd ABN/D. François.)

Gavin with his 505th PIR will be the spearhead of the 82nd during Operation Husky. (Ph. 82nd ABN/D. François.)

marches, desert orienteering courses, night grouping after a parachute simulation and landing in gliders, construction of shelters and foxholes, laying of mine fields at dawn, etc. These training exercises were designed to prepare the men for imminent operations.

On June 16, 1943, the advanced units of the division were taken by truck to the Tunisian frontier, towards Kairouan. From June 21 and until July 6, all the paratroopers of the division were airlifted to regroup with the advanced unit.

Training started up again, in a more favorable environment, even though it was still very hot. The paratroopers discovered the battlefields which had witnessed fighting between the British and Rommel's Afrika Korps. Morale was very high, the "All American" paratroopers felt ready for action.

The long-awaited moment came on July 9, 1943. That very evening, the 505th PIR, 456th PFAB and Co "B" of the 307th AEB and the 3rd Battalion of the 504th PIR boarded the planes that would take them to Sicily.

Troops embarking. (Ph. D. François.)

A para from the 505th waiting to embark, under the wing of a C-47. (Ph. 82nd ABN/D. François.)

Patton, Bradley Ridgway and Taylor in North Africa. (Ph. 82nd ABN/D. François.)

Men from the 504th PIR a few minutes before embarking. (Ph. 82nd ABN/D. François.)

Colonel Tucker of the 504th PIR before embarking for Sicily. (Ph. 82nd ABN/D. François.)

Sicily

The code name for the operation was "Husky". The objective was to land in Sicily then set up a strong bridgehead. Its loss was to be a serious blow to the Axis Forces in the sector, and later in Italy. This Italian island was the key to the Mediterranean and the "front door" into Europe. Husky was the first in a series of operations, proceeding like a cascade of dominos, to be followed by other landing operations in Italy, Provence and Normandy.

After several months training, the date of June 9, 1943 was chosen for the operation, since there would be a full moon to illuminate the drop zones.

The initial phase of the operation consisted in parachuting two airborne divisions, one British and the other American. The first objective was to secure a beachhead ready for the arrival of the land forces and avoid a German counter-attack during the vulnerable period when the first troops would be landing. Under the code name "Ladbroke", the English red berets of the 1st Airborne Division were assigned the Syracuse sector in the south east of the island. The 82nd Airborne Division was assigned the Gela sector, further west.

Due to the shortage of transport aircraft, the first wave consisted of only one reinforced regiment. The first jump was made by Colonel Gavin leading the 505th PIR, reinforced by the 3rd Battalion of Colonel Tucker's 504th PIR, who were given the mission of clearing the way by jumping first.

The following night, Tucker's two remaining battalions together with 376th PFAB and Co "C" of the 307th AEB had to jump and join up with their comrades. The operation was code-named "Husky II".

The drop zone (DZ) for "Husky I" was located in a mountainous area a few kilometers east of Gela.

From the outset, the planners feared that the para-

Here, like everywhere in Europe, civilians are the first victims of the combats. (Ph. NA/D. François.)

troopers of the 505th would be unable to reach their objectives "X" and "Y". Objective "X", located near the town of Nescemi, in the north east of Gela, was assigned to the 3rd Battalion of the 504th PIR. The 505th would have to take control of a road junction located to the east of Gela, which was extremely well protected by a system of fortifications and machine gun nests.

Columns of prisoners can be seen everywhere, following the Allied advance. (Ph. NA/D. François.)

Above: tanks going through Italian villages. (Ph. NA/D. François.)

Below: prisoners of war penned in temporary camps. (Ph. NA/D. François.)

After checking their equipment for the nth time, the paratroopers in the first wave were split up over 10 different airfields before taking off. 266 aircraft took to the skies at 23h15. To avoid friendly fire from the hundreds of ships heading for the landing zone, the formations had to take complicated dog-leg courses running from the African coast towards Malta, before turning sharply north towards the south west tip of Sicily.

The C-47s then had to fly over the sea again, to avoid fire from the enemy coastal batteries. They had to cover a total of more than 370 miles (600 km) to reach the drop zone. To avoid being detected by the Germans, they had to fly at an altitude of less than 230 feet (70 m) above the sea, then climb to a height of 650 feet (200 m) during the drop phase.

Things went wrong right from the start. The English gliders flying towards their landing zones (LZ) in the Syracuse sector came under by friendly fire. 90 gliders came down in the sea. In addition, the Army meteorologists has forecast a 30 mph (50 km/h) crosswind over the drop zones, which was much higher than usual. During training, jumps were canceled when the wind speed exceeded 15 mph (25 km/h). The aircraft were scattered over the Mediterranean and did not see the landmarks on Malta, some aircraft turned back, others decided to head towards Sicily relying on dead-reckoning. Because of these errors and the wind speed, the paratroopers of the 82nd were dropped in utter confusion and scattered

over vast sectors of land. Colonel Gavin and his men landed over 19 miles (30 km) east of their planned drop zone. The last of Gavin's paratroopers to jump landed at 01h00 on July 10. Only 15 % of the troops reached their drop zone.

On the ground, the men tried to regroup by stick or unit. Some managed to form groups of several hundred men, but many found themselves alone behind the enemy lines.

Out of the 3405 paratroopers who took part in Husky I, 4 hours after the drop Gavin was only able to regroup 20 men. Of all the units dropped that night, the 2nd Battalion of the 505th PIR commanded by Major Mark Alexander was the only one which managed to stay grouped.

In spite of all these incidents, the objectives were reached. Objective "X" (Nescemi) was taken by the men of the 3rd Battalion of the 504th PIR and objective "Y" was captured by men from Co "A" led by Captain Sayre of the 505th.

Alone or in groups, the paratroopers of the 82nd executed their missions, disrupting enemy communication lines and preventing a counter-attack against the four American divisions landing on the beaches.

Amongst the defeats inflicted on the enemy, the action carried out by the one hundred men led by Lt. Col. Arthur Gorham of the 1st Battalion, 505th Regiment, has remained one of the most important feats of arms that occurred during this operation. They managed to overcome paratroopers from the Hermann Goering Division, moving from the south to their base at Caltagirone, from where their intention was to counter-attack the landing forces. Armed with nothing more than two 60-mm mortars and two light

Sherman tanks stopped in an Italian village. (Ph. NA/D. François.)

After landing, the Allies now advance towards the north of Italy. (Ph. NA/D. François.)

machine guns, Gorham's men attacked an enemy strongpoint. In the ensuing fighting, 40 Italian soldiers and 10 Germans surrendered. 15 men were later found dead inside the bastion. Using captured enemy weapons and information obtained from the prisoners, the men from the 505th prepared to face the paratroopers of the Hermann Goering Division. After destroying two Panzer-Grenadier companies, several vehicles and 2 tanks, the 1st Battalion were forced to pull back to new positions where they continued fighting. The action carried out by this handful of men gave the troops landing on the beaches several hours respite.

Another desperate action took place on July 11, 1943, with Colonel Gavin and 180 men he had finally managed to group together. Many belonged to Lt. Col. Krause's 3rd Battalion. The small unit stopped a combat group of the Hermann Goering Panzer-Division, that was attempting to break through the exposed flank of the 45th American Infantry Division and drive them back into the sea. Apart from this group of paratroopers from the 82nd, at first the enemy encountered no American resistance as it moved forward. The small force from the 3rd Battalion held a defensive position on Biazza Ridge. The Ridge was the scene of fierce fighting between the two groups. Although outnumbered, Gavin's men managed to hold their positions. Firmly dug in, the small group fought throughout the day, with no hopes of reinforcements. By chance, Captain Al Ireland from the 505th regiment was able to report the desperate situation of Gavin and his men to General Bradley and General Troy Middletown, who called up a 155 mm artillery barrage to relieve the little group. The artillery support, combined with the fierce determination of this brave paratroopers, not only stopped the German attack on the flank, but also helped protect the American troops advancing inland.

Tragedy strikes

During the night of D+1 (July 10-11), the 504th (without its 3rd Battalion) led by Colonel Reuben H. Tucker boarded the C-47s stationed in the Kairouan sector to take part in the second operation. The night was calmer than during the first drop and lit by a crescent moon. The drop zone was behind the position occupied by the 1st Infantry Division. Everyone expected an uneventful flight.

Sadly, the outcome proved to be quite different, and one of the greatest tragedies in the history of airborne troops was about to strike.

The US invasion fleet, off the Sicilian coast, was on alert, enemy aircraft had been sighted and had already suffered an air attack. As the formations of the 504th regiment heading towards their drop zones were passing over the fleet, a gunner on one of the vessels opened fire, mistaking the friendly troop carriers for German fighters. This was in spite of the fact that Ridgway had received confirmation that the Navy had been informed and would withhold fire. 23 aircraft were shot down by friendly fire, 81 troopers were killed, including Ridgway's assistant, General Keerans. It was a disaster. The rest of the formation was scattered to the four winds in a sky lit up by anti-aircraft fire.

On July 18, the division moved west to Patton's sector, to clean up western Sicily. The towns of Agrigento, Licata, St.Marguerita and Castelvetrano were taken by the 82nd. The division suffered few casualties, but took 23 000 prisoners. In five days, the 82nd Airborne Division advanced more than 125 miles (200 km).

The 82nd occupied western Sicily for two weeks. On August 17, Messina was captured and the division relieved from its duties as occupation force. On the 19th, the division started to head back to Kairouan in Tunisia, to prepare for a new mission, the invasion of Italy.

Italy

During the Casablanca conference in January 1943, the Allies had agreed on the need to invade southern

Combat engineers on mine clearance operations around these wrecked Panzers. (Ph. NA/D. François.)

Italy. It was strategically important to force the Italian government to withdraw from the conflict and pull German forces away from the Eastern front and the coasts in Northern France where a landing had already been planned in Normandy.

Now that the Allies controlled Sicily and the Mediterranean, they were in a position to consider attacking Italy.

Numerous plans were drawn up to invade Italy, the 82nd being one of the key elements in the operation. Each time, however, the mission was cancelled. One of these plans consisted in dropping the 82nd over Rome to join the anti-Fascist Italian troops. A secret mission was even carried out by General Maxwell Taylor, then commanding the Division artillery, to meet Marshall Badoglio. The meeting failed to come up with a joint plan since the opposition army was completely disorganized. Badoglio was unable to guarantee that the airports required by the invading troops could be taken. The mission was called off at the last minute, with the troopers of the 82nd already on board the aircraft.

On September 13, 1943, General Ridgway received an urgent request for support from General Mark Clark, commanding the 5th Army. General Clark needed immediate reinforcement to support his troops which had been landing at Salerno since September 9.

At 23h26, the same day, less than 15 hours after General Clark's request, the 1st and 2nd Battalions of the 504th with 2 sections of Co "C" from the 307th Airborne Engineer Battalion attached, jumped onto a small drop zone on the Paestrum beachhead. This operation saw the advent of a new unit whose role was to mark the drop zone: the Pathfinders. For their first mission, the Pathfinders were equipped with beacons to guide the main airborne force (Eureka transmitters and Rebecca receivers in the aircraft) and equipment to mark out the drop zone for the main troops. The result was immediate, most paratroopers landed within 200 yards of the drop zone and the farthest about half a mile away.

On September 15, the 325th GIR and the 3rd Battalion of the 504th landed on the Salerno beaches (Seaborne) to reinforce the left flank of the 6th Corps.

On September 16, the 1st and 2nd Battalions of the 504th PIR attacked the high ground at Altavilla. The next day, they were surrounded and under heavy enemy fire. General Dawley, Commander of the 6th Corps, suggested that the 504th should withdraw. Colonel Tucker vehemently replied: "Retreat, hell! Send me my 3rd Battalion!" After a forced march, the 3rd Battalion reached Altavilla to rejoin its regiment. Later on, the General was to say that this operation had saved the Salerno bridgehead.

The next night, the 505th led by Colonel James Gavin, together with Co "B" of the 307th Airborne Engineer Battalion, jumped to the right of the positions held by the 504th.

In the meantime, the 325th GIR was fighting in the Sorrentine peninsula alongside the 3rd Battalion of the 504th and Ranger units.

Another parachute battalion was attached to the 82nd Airborne Division for this operation, the 509th PIR. The 509th jumped in the Avellino sector located about 18 miles (30 kilometers) from Salerno, in a very mountainous region, highly unsuitable for parachuting.

Throughout the month of September, the 82nd continued fighting in the Salerno and Naples sectors. The 505th PIR took the town of Pompeii and was the first unit to enter Naples.

During this period, Gavin was promoted to Brigadier General, becoming General Ridgway's assistant.

The division remained in Naples during the entire month of October as occupation force. This offered opportunity for the men to take some well-earned rest. Since their arrival in North Africa, there had been very little time for relaxation.

In the mountains, the 504th PIR was still fighting. The men were in action on Mount Sammucro and the neighboring mountains in the Venafro sector. After 19 days fighting, the 504th was finally able to leave the front and go to Naples to rest and prepare for further missions.

On November 18, the 82nd Airborne Division, without the 504th PIR, set off for Ireland in order to prepare for the landing in France. The 504th and 509th stayed in Italy to reinforce the 5th Army. The two units fought in the mountains and became experts in patrolling mountainous regions.

German prisoner of war parachutists. (Ph. NA/D. François.)

Two dead American soldiers covered with flowers laid by Italian civilians. (Ph. NA/D. François.)

The GI's are enthusiastically welcomed by Sicilian and Italian civilians.(Ph. NA/D. François.)

Anzio

The *504th PIR* continued fighting in the Venafro sector, before being relieved on December 27. By January 22, 1944, the regiment was back in action, as part of the 5th Army for the assault on Anzio.

The 504th landed on Anzio beach and took up position on the right flank of the bridgehead, along the Mussolini Canal. The 3rd Battalion fought in the northern sector where it earned the *Presidential Unit Citation* for its heroic action in the town of Aprilia.

It was during that period that the paratroopers were nicknamed the « *Devils in Baggy Pants* ». During the Anzio campaign, the 504th fought against elements of the Hermann Goering division, the 16th *SS-Panzergrenadier-Division* and the *3rd Panzergrenadier-Division*.

The 504th was finally withdrawn from Anzio on March 25, 1944, and set sail for England to join the 82nd Airborne Division once again.

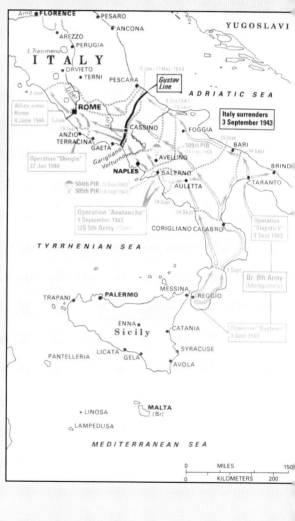

During the Sicily campaign, paratroopers of the 82nd use mules to carry their equipment. (Ph. 82nd ABN/D. François.)

Prisoner of war, veteran of the Afrika Korps. (Ph. NA/D. François.)

Faced with the lack of transport in Sicily, the paratroopers recover enemy vehicles. (Ph. 82nd ABN/D. François.)

The first armored vehicles arrive in Sicily. (Ph. 82nd ABN/D. François.)

The paratroopers advance in the Sicilian villages. (Ph. 82nd ABN/D. François.)

257 + 16

Ridgway and his staff in Sicily. (Ph. 82nd ABN/D. François.)

Gliders from the 325th GIR returning to England. (Ph. D. François.)

General Ridgway, commanding the 82nd in Sicily, in his jeep. (Ph. 82nd ABN/D. François.)

Ridgway in the third row in Sicily, note his "Mickey" camouflage helmet, typical of Sicily. (Ph. 82nd ABN/D. François.)

C-47s taking off for Salerme. (Ph. NA/D. François.)

Paratroopers from the 82nd enter Naples. (Ph. 82nd ABN/D. François.)

Paratroopers from the *505th PIR* back at Tripoli after the drop in Sicily. (Ph. 82nd ABN/D. François.)

The paratroopers enter Naples. (Ph. 82nd ABN/D. François.)

Men from the 82nd Airborne Division are taken by boat to England. (Ph. D. François.)

—World-Herald Photo by John Savage, Transmitted by AP Wirephoto.

The tradition that "The Old Flag shall never hit the ground" is upheld under great strain here. Lt. Horace J. Cofer successfully struggles to hold the Stars and Stripes aloft while collapsing his chute during the re-enactment of the invasion of Sicily before 62 thousand spectators at Alliance, ., Sunday. In the demonstration, in which glider-borne troops took part at the dedication of the nce air base, Lt. Cofer dropped out of the skies carrying the colors with him.

cily Invasion Re-Enacted Before 62,000
as Air Base at Alliance Is Dedicated

y Lawrence Youngman
(World-Herald Staff Member.)
iance, Neb.—The flying and
ng men at the Alliance air
Sunday dished out a terrific
icling to "Little Sicily,'" cap-
g the enemy's airdrome as 62
and persons looked on.
e re-enactment of the Sicily
ion featured ceremonies dedi-
g the Alliance base.
st came the big four-motored
ers, flying in tight formation

at eight thousand feet and dropping fragmentation bombs to
knock out imaginary aircraft and
anti-aircraft guns and to paste
ground troops.
Then the lighter bombers poured
on more bombs, and cut loose with
their machine guns. More soften-
ing up. Next came the fast, wicked
combat planes like mad hornets.
Then the troop carrier planes
came in, loaded with parachute
infantry soldiers, and with parachute equipment, in what the soldiers call "parapacks."

First out of the big planes were
the bundles of equipment—the
chutes are in brilliant colors, and
each color identifies the weapon
and supplies the bundle contains.
First to hit the ground were the
light .30-caliber machine guns—
not the best weapons in the world
but held ideal for the immediate
job of seizing a "bridgehead."
Then the paratroopers came in.
The snowy parachutes billowed
out of the planes in "sticks" of
(Continued on Page 4, Column 1.)

Press article of an American newspaper relating the fighting in Sicily. (Coll. D. François.)

Paratroopers from the 82nd enjoy a short break in Naples. (Ph. 82nd ABN/D. François.)

Explosion at the Naples post office. (Ph. 82nd ABN/D. François.)

The paratroopers advance under the cover of olive trees. (Ph. 82nd ABN/D. François.

Men from company « C » of the 307th repairing a bridge in Italy. (Ph. 82nd ABN/D. François.)

Men from company « C » of the 307th repairing a bridge in Italy. (Ph. 82nd ABN/D. François.)

General James Gavin and the war correspondent Jack B. Thompson in Sicily. (Ph. 82nd ABN/D. François.)

117

Paratroopers from the 82nd advancing along roads in Italy. (Ph. 82nd ABN/D. François.)

The Allies land at Anzio. (Ph. 82nd ABN/D. François.)

Daniel B. MacIlvoy from the 505th PIR at Naples. (Ph. 82nd ABN/D. François.)

Men from the engineer battalion clearing mines on Anzio beach. (Ph. NA/D. François.)

General Mark Clark, commanding the 5th Army.

Prisoners of war. (Ph. NA/D. François.)

General Clark likes to fly over the battlefield in his observation airplane. (Ph. NA/D. François.)

Paratroopers from the 504th will fight for more than 8 weeks on the Anzio bridgehead along the Mussolini Canal. (Ph. 82nd ABN/D. François.)

General Mark Clark, commanding the 5th Army. Prisoners of war. (Ph. NA/D. François.)

American armored vehicles arriving in Rome. (Ph. NA/D. François.)

Paratroopers from the 82nd setting up an 81 mm mortar. (Ph. 82nd ABN/D. François.)

The *508th* land in Northern Ireland. (Ph. D. François.)

Northern Ireland/England
Plans and missions

The 82nd arrived in Ireland on December 9, 1943. In the meantime, *Brigadier General* James Gavin*, Assistant Division Commander*, had been appointed advisor for Operation *Overlord*, in its airborne phase, code-named Neptune.

On General Ridgway's insistence, the 82nd was to be reinforced by two parachute regiments from the 2nd Airborne Infantry Brigade, commanded by General George Howell. This brigade consisted of two parachute infantry regiments, the *507th* and the *508th*, which were to replace the *504th PIR*, unable to take part in Neptune because of its depleted ranks.

The division was then transferred to England in February where it resumed training. The *401st GIR* was attached to the *325th PIR* to increase the number of troops arriving by glider.

On May 26, 1944, all the plans and missions were assigned to the 82nd division, which had been attached to the *First Army*. A series of maps was issued to the regiment commanders and battalion majors. The elements which would have to land on the beaches *(Seaborne)* were transferred to the assembly areas on the south coasts of England, while waiting to embark.

The 82nd Division was assigned the following mission :

« *Land by parachute and glider before and after dawn of D-Day west of Saint-Sauveur le Vicomte, seize,* clear and secure the sector of St.Jacques de Nehou – Besneville – Saint-Sauveur-Le-Vicomte, seize and blow up the Sangsurière bridges at Saint-Sauveur-de-Pierrepont, etc. »

The mission was changed by the *First Army* commander further to reports supplied by military intelligence confirming significant enemy forces in the Saint-Sauveur-le-Vicomte sector, with the 91st Infantry Division.

Although the mission of the 82nd was unchanged, the sites selected were modified. It became :

« *Land by parachute and glider before and after dawn of D-Day around the river Merderet, seize, clear and secure the following sectors: Neuville au Plain, Baudienville, capture Sainte-Mère-Eglise, seize and secure the crossings above the Merderet, at La Fière and Chef du Pont and set up a bridgehead. Destroy the crossings of the Douve river at Beuzeville la Bastille and Etienville. Protect the northwest flank of the 7th Corps.*

Following these new orders and administrative details, the division's staff had to quickly modify the operation plans. Luckily, these changes of location did not affect the basic plan, the operation had three phases, corresponding to the intervention of 3 forces:

Force "A", commanded by *Brigadier General* James M. Gavin, which would jump at dawn on D-Day, comprising :

Units :	Aircraft
Detachment 82nd A/B Div HQ & HQ Co	4
Pathfinders	9
Det. HQ 82nd A/B Div Artillery	2
Det. 82nd A/B Div Signal Corps	3
Det. 456th Parachute FA Battalion (attached to the 505th)	
Air Support (attached to the HQ 82nd A/B Div.)	
505th Parachute Infantry Regiment	117
507th Parachute Infantry Regiment	117
508th Parachute Infantry Regiment	117
Co « B », 307th A/B Engineer Battalion	9
Total :	**378**

Force « B », commanded by *Major General* Matthew B. Ridgway, commanding the division, which would arrive in gliders after dawn on D-Day, including :

Units :	Gliders
82nd A/B Div HQ & HQ Co	22
HQ & HQ Battery, 82nd A/B Div Artillery	11
82nd A/B Div Signal Corps	13
325th Glider Infantry Regiment	172
319th Glider Field Artillery Battalion	40
320th Glider Field Artillery Battalion	54
Batteries A, B, C, 80th Airborne AA Battalion	57

Unit	
Co « A », 307th A/B Engineer Battalion	10
307th Airborne Medical Co	20
82nd Airborne Recon Platoon	13
Air Support	4
Command vehicles - Parachute regiments	12
Total :	**428**

Force "C" commanded by Brigadier General George P.Howell, commanding the 2nd Airborne Infantry Brigade, which would arrive by sea and land between D+2 and D+7, including:

456th Field Artillery Battalion
80th Airborne Antiaircraft Battalion
307th Airborne Engineer Battalion
782nd Airborne Ord. Maintenance Co.
407th Airborne Quarter Master Co.
82nd Airborne Military Police Platoon
Corps Medical Dets.
87th Armored FA Battalion (attached)
899th Tank Destroyer Field Artillery Battalion (attached)
Tr B, 4th Cav. Squadron (attached)
Co "C", 746th Tank Battalion (attached)
3809 QM Trk Co (attached)
3810 QM Trk Co (attached)
1st Platoon, 603rd QM Co (attached)

Demonstration jump in England. (Ph. NA/D. François.)

Under the plan, Force « A » was to approach the Cotentin Peninsula from the west and drop between 01h00 and 03h15, on the night of D/D+1, on three drop zones. The *505th PIR* and its attachments were to land east of the Merderet river, about 1000 yards northwest of Sainte-Mère-Eglise. The *507th PIR* was to land west of the Merderet river, about 1000 yards from Amfreville. The *508th PIR* and the Force « A » headquarters were to land west of the Merderet river, about 1000 yards north of Picauville.

52 gliders of Force « B » were to approach the Cotentin from the west prior to H-hour and land on the *505th PIR* drop zone. The remainder of Force « B » was to approach the peninsula from the east and was to land on the *landing zones* between Sainte-Mère-Eglise and Blosville.

In a last-minute change of plan, General Ridgway decided to parachute with Force « A ».

Aerial resupply missions were scheduled for the morning of D+1 if needed by the ground troops.

All elements of the division had reached the assembly areas 24 hours before H-hour. Various airfields in the south of England were chosen for the paratroopers, in the sectors of Grantham, Cottesmore and Langar. The gliders were at seven airfields in the sectors of Aldermaston, Ramsbury and Merryfield.

All men were briefed on their missions on June 4 in the morning, all the equipment was rechecked. Unfortunately at the last minute, while the paratroopers were waiting on the taxi ways to embark, the operation was postponed 24 hours because of bad weather conditions along the shores of the Channel.

The first planes of Force « A » took off at 23h15 on June 5, taking with them the pathfinders who would mark out the drop zones, starting the largest airborne operation of all time.

The 13,000 paratroopers forming the 82nd and 101st Airborne Divisions followed behind.

Paratroopers from the *508th PIR* have set up headquarters at Nottingham. (Ph. D. François.)

The British Prime Minister, Winston Churchill, meets the paratroopers from the two *American Airborne Divisions* which were to jump in Normandy a few weeks later. (Ph. NA/D. François.)

Bivouac camp at Nottingham in Wollaton park. (Ph. D. François.)

Paratroopers from the *508th PIR* leave the port of New York en route for Northern Ireland. (Ph. D. François.)

Lieutenant Malcolm Brannen from the *508th PIR* at Nottingham. In a few weeks time, he was to jump at Picauville in Normandy and kill the German General Wilhem Falley. (Ph. D. François.)

City of Nottingham.

THE LORD MAYOR (Councillor F. Mitchell)

AND THE CORPORATION

request the pleasure of the company of

Lt. Colonel William Kuhn.

AT LUNCHEON

AT THE COUNCIL HOUSE

on THURSDAY, 23RD MARCH, at 12.45 for 1 p.m.

to meet

OFFICERS AND MEN OF

THE UNITED STATES ARMY.

Please reply to :
The Lord Mayor's Secretary,
The Council House,
Nottingham.

Invitation card sent to Lt. Colonel William Kuhn from the *507th PIR* by the Mayor of Nottingham. (Coll. *507th PIR* Ass.)

A paratrooper from the 508th at Nottingham. (Ph. D. François.)

The Americans make friends with their British cousins. (Ph. D. François.)

Above: Sergeant MacGrath from the *508th PIR* on the ship taking him to Northern Ireland. (Ph. D. François.)

Opposite: the paratroopers from the 82nd were to spend several months in bivouac camps, while waiting for Operation Neptune. (Ph. D. François.)

Below: Wollaton Park at Nottingham, where the 507th and 508th were to spend the months leading up to D-Day in a bivouac camp. (Ph. D. François.)

Lt. Malcolm Brannen from the *508th PIR*. (Ph. D. François.)

Nottingham. These paratroopers are resting near a city made famous in the Middle Ages by its Sheriff, at the time of John « Lackland » and the King Richard the Lionheart. Firearms have replaced the longbows of Robin Hood and his comrades… (Ph. D. François.)

The Mayor and the Sheriff of Nottingham meet Colonel Millett (*507th PIR*) and Colonel Lindquist (*508th PIR*). (Ph. D. François.)

Le Maire et le Shérif de Nottingham rencontrent le colonel Millett *(507th PIR)* et le colonel Lindquist *(508th PIR)*. (Ph. D. François.)

Officers from the *507th PIR* receive an enthusiastic welcome by the population of Nottingham. (Ph. D. François.)

Men from the *507th PIR* boarding for a practice jump. Second from the left, *Sgt.* O'neil Boe. (Ph. D. François.)

Men from the *507th PIR* boarding for a practice jump. Second from the left, Sgt. O'neil Boe. (Ph. D. François.)

Officials visit the airborne troops stationed in England. (Ph. Marty Morgan.)

Paratroopers from the 507th PIR on parade at Port Steward in Northern Ireland. (Ph. D. François.)

On June 5, 1944, C-47s and gliders line up ready to take off, destination: Normandy. (Ph. D. François.)

Riggers sections repair the parachutes. (Ph. NA/D. François.)

Captain Roy Creek from the 507th PIR marches proudly at the head of his company in Northern Ireland. (Ph. D. François.)

A paratrooper from the *508th PIR* posing with a bazooka. Nottingham, May 1944. (Ph. D. François.)

The machine guns are oiled ready for Operation Neptune. (Ph. D. François.)

1. Paratroopers from the *507th PIR* with the Mayor and the Sheriff of Nottingham. (Ph. D. François.)

2. Sgt. Frank Staples from the *508th PIR* en route for England in January 1944. (Ph. D. François.)

3. Two infantrymen from the *325th GIR* : Henri Joseph Hirleman, who was to become a Pathfinder in Holland, and Russell Andermann, who was to participate in the Battle of La Fière in a few months time. (Ph. D. François.)

Frank Staples during a practice jump in the United States. (Ph. D. François.)

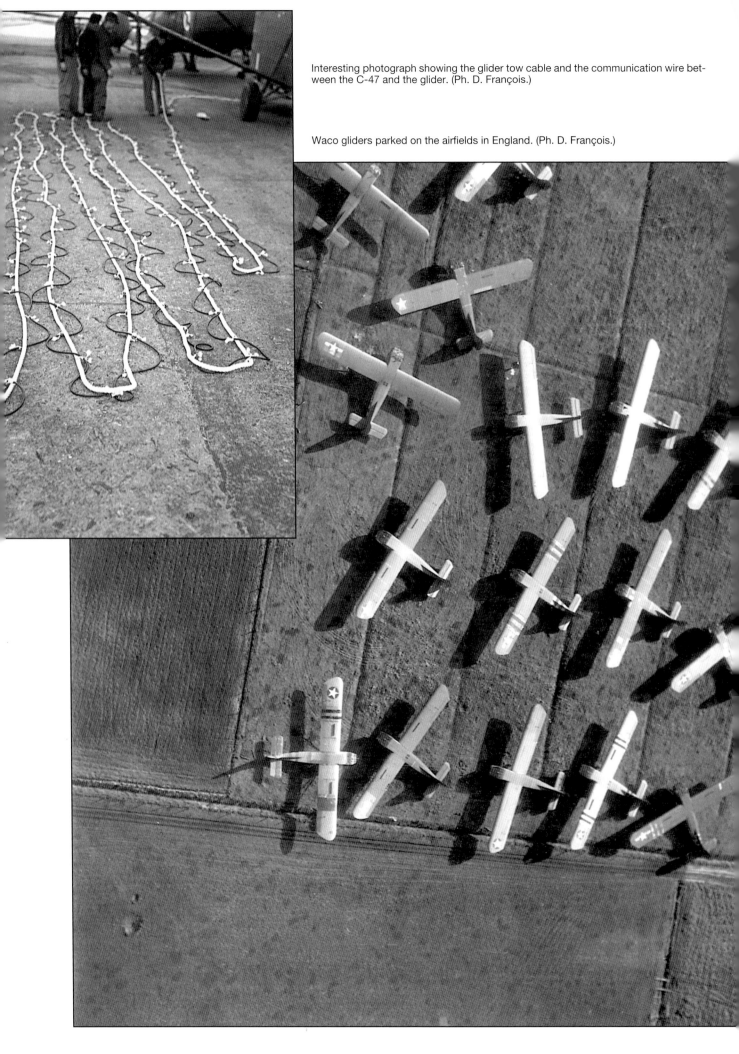

Interesting photograph showing the glider tow cable and the communication wire between the C-47 and the glider. (Ph. D. François.)

Waco gliders parked on the airfields in England. (Ph. D. François.)

140

Lieutenant-colonel Maloney from the 507th PIR. (Ph. D. François.)

Waco CG-4A glider. (Ph. D. François.)

Paratroopers from the *508th PIR* in front of Nottingham town hall. (Ph. D. François.)

A few weeks before D-Day, the paratroopers from the two American divisions return one of their jump suits to the Riggers sections so that some parts of the suits, too fragile for hedge warfare, can be reinforced. These two paratroopers have just received them. In the background, a pile of reinforced jump suits. (Ph. NA/D. François.)

SUPREME HEADQUARTERS
ALLIED EXPEDITIONARY FORCE

TO ALL MEMBERS OF THE ALLIED EXPEDITIONARY FORCE:

The task which we set ourselves is finished, and the time has come for me to relinquish Combined Command.

In the name of the United States and the British Commonwealth, from whom my authority is derived, I should like to convey to you the gratitude and admiration of our two nations for the manner in which you have responded to every demand that has been made upon you. At times, conditions have been hard and the tasks to be performed arduous. No praise is too high for the manner in which you have surmounted every obstacle.

I should like, also, to add my own personal word of thanks to each one of you for the part you have played, and the contribution you have made to our joint victory.

Now that you are about to pass to other spheres of activity, I say Good-bye to you and wish you Good Luck and God-Speed.

Dwight Eisenhower

Message from General Eisenhower distributed to the troops landing in Normandy. (Coll. D. François.)

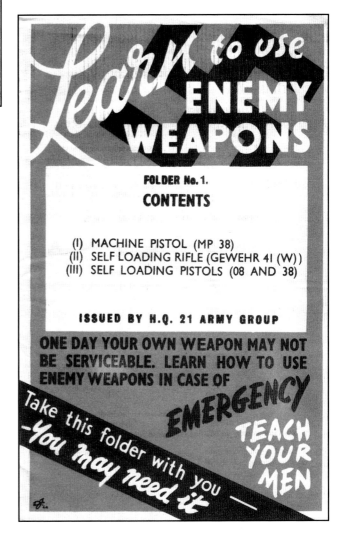

Enemy weapon user manual distributed to the paratroopers. (Coll. D. François.)

Riggers are responsible for repairing the parachutes. (Ph. NA/D. François.)

Men from the airborne artillery prepare the Howitzers and their munitions, which will be dropped with them over Normandy. (Ph. 82nd ABN/D. François.)

Riggers sections repair the parachutes. (Ph. NA/D. François.)

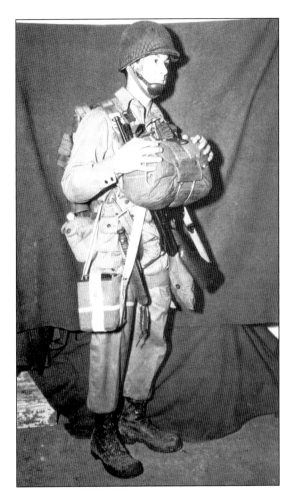

These Waco gliders have not yet been camouflaged with their invasion paint. (Ph. D. François.)

A *Pathfinder* showing the beacon equipment he will need to mark out the jump zones in Normandy. (Ph. NA/D. François.)

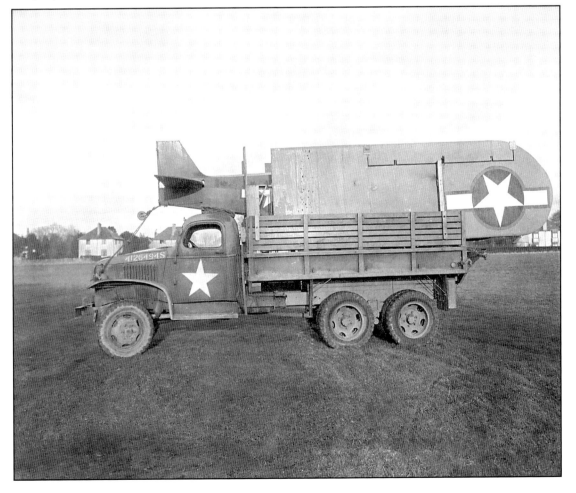

Transport of a Waco glider, sent in crates from the United States. (Ph. NA/D. François.)

MacGrath from the 508th PIR resting in his tent at Wollaton Park. In a few weeks time, he was to jump in Normandy. (Ph. D. François.)

Some units from the 82nd embarking on the ships with the landing force. (Ph. NA/D. François.)

O'Neil Boe from the 507th PIR aiming a 60 mm mortar. (Ph. D. François.)

O'Neil Boe. (Ph. D. François.)

Team of *Pathfinders* from the *505th PIR*. (Ph. NA/D. François.)

Team of Pathfinders from the *505th PIR*. (Ph. NA/D. François.)

Bottom of page photographs: team of *Pathfinders* from the *505th PIR*. (Ph. NA/D. François.)

Team of *Pathfinders* from the *507th PIR*. (Ph. NA/D. François.)

Team of Pathfinders from the *507th PIR*. (Ph. NA/D. François.)

Team of Pathfinders from the *508th PIR*. (Ph. NA/D. François.)

Teams of Pathfinders from the *508th PIR*. (Ph. NA/D. François.)

1. Paratroopers from the *508th PIR* preparing their equipment before being transferred to airfields in the south of England. (Ph. D. François.)

3

2 and **3.** nfantrymen from the *325th GIR* on board their glider, heading for Normandy. (Ph. 82nd ABN/D. François.)

4. Infantrymen from the *325th* on the edge of the runways waiting for the order to board the aircraft. (Ph. 82nd ABN/D. François.)

4

The *325th Glider Infantry Regiment* boarding the aircraft. The men are grouped near the gliders before boarding shortly afterwards. (Ph. 82nd ABN/D. François.)

Paratroopers from the *82nd Airborne Division board* Dakotas on June 5, 1944, at about 22h30. Some are strapping on their harnesses. (Ph. D. François.)

The *325th Glider Infantry Regiment* boarding the aircraft. (Ph. 82nd ABN/D. François.)

Paratroopers from the *508th PIR* putting on their equipment. Compare with the photograph at the top of page 155. (Ph. NA/D. François.)

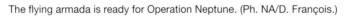

The flying armada is ready for Operation Neptune. (Ph. NA/D. François.)

Paratroopers from the *508th PIR* check their parachutes. (Ph. NA/D. François.)

Paratroopers from the *508th PIR* writing their last letters. (Ph. NA/D. François.)

The intelligence section of the *508th PIR*, a few hours before embarking for Normandy. Note that many of them have been issued a Thompson machine gun. (Ph. D. François.)

The paratroopers have blackened their faces for camouflage before the night jump over Normandy. (Ph. D. François.)

Normandy

« *...33 days of action without relief, without replacements. Every mission accomplished. No ground gained was ever relinquished.* »

Major General Matthew B. Ridgway

The flight over the English channel passed without incident and the various formations regrouped, even though the sky seemed to be full of troop transport planes and fighters. Down below, the fleet and its thousands of ships traveled over a rough sea, not at all suited for a landing.

The various markers, used for navigation by the C-47 pilots, were at the meeting point. Even a submarine was used as a marker in order to give the exact axis of penetration over the Cotentin peninsula.

On approaching the coasts, an extremely thick mist and then anti-aircraft fire scattered the formations, which had to drop their sticks in very poor conditions: excessively high drop speed, low altitude and, above all, far from the planned drop zones.

Meanwhile, similar confusion reigned on the German side, with the dispersion of the Americans making a counter-offensive complicated. It was impossible to determine the scale of the American forces, maybe an isolated commando operation or perhaps a wider-ranging offensive.

The night was to be a tragic one for many men caught up by their fate, including two general officers, one German and one American.

The Pathfinders

The first Pathfinders of the *82nd Airborne Division* landed in Normandy at 00h30.

A last coffee with a donut, before embarking for Normandy. (Ph. D. François.)

The three teams of Pathfinders from the *505th PIR* landed at their drop zone (DZ « O ») located close to Sainte-Mère-Eglise.

The Pathfinders of the *507th PIR*, meanwhile, landed in a zone occupied by the enemy (DZ « T »). It was under heavy fire, therefore, that Lt. Ames' operators installed a single Eureka beacon, although they were unable to mark out the land using their lamps.

The teams of the *508th PIR* (DZ « N ») to the west of the river Merderet (the village of Gueutteville) had no better a landing. Lt. Gene Williams and one of his men landed near Pont-l'Abbé and only managed to install a single Eureka beacon and two lamps.

Since the formations were dispersed, most of the Pathfinders teams did not know where they were, and certain equipment did not seem to be working. In short, the night-time operation seemed to be off to a bad start.

Drop Zone «O»

The plan was for the 1st Battalion of Colonel William Ekman's 505th to go from their drop zone (DZ « O ») and take the end of the La Fière roadway, where a bridge passed over the Merderet. Only one company, Co «A», was able to complete the mission. The other side of the roadway was supposed to be held by the 507th.

The roadway was a road lined with trees and surrounded by flooded areas. To the east, the La Fière bridge bordered a farm, known as the La Fière Manor.

The 1st Battalion had been dispersed during the jump and many paratroopers were located on opposite sides of the river Merderet. By chance, Lt. John

Dolan's Co « A » quickly crossed back over the Merderet, helped by Co «C» and by some paratroopers of the 507th, and launched an assault on the La Fière farm where German soldiers had established a strongpoint.

Now occupying the farm and the east bank of the Merderet, Dolan prepared a defense of the square. During the day, the Germans organized a counter-offensive in the direction of the La Fière bridge, led by three Renault tanks from Picauville. From their individual foxholes, two Bazooka teams opened fire, destroying the three enemy armored vehicles. The enemy retreated, leaving three wrecked vehicles burnt out on the roadway.

The 2nd Battalion of the 505th landed under good conditions, with their pathfinders able to correctly mark out the drop zone (*27 of the 36 sticks landed either on the DZ or very close to it*). However Lt. Col. Benjamin Vandervoort, commander of the battalion, injured his ankle on landing and had to lead his unit whilst seated in an ammunition cart. He took the Neuville-Au-Plain road in order to take the northern access to Sainte-Mère-Eglise on the RN13 highway. Meanwhile, Lt. Col. Edward Krause and his 3rd Battalion took the Sainte-Mère-Eglise road, with the objective of taking the village at dawn. Four groups were put together and sent in different directions to reconnoiter the terrain, with orders to be back within 45 minutes. The reconnaissance groups returned with a group of 90 paratroopers guided by a visibly drunk Frenchman, who revealed to them that the enemy infantry battalion which had been in the barracks in the village a week previously was now outside Sainte-Mère-Eglise, in the camps of a transport and administration unit (in the village of Fauville). Krause quickly reorganized his unit into two companies and marched towards the village, sheltered by the hedgerows. Arriving at the outskirts of Sainte-Mère, he ordered six sections to block different accesses to the village, with the exception of the access route he planned on using himself. After allowing time for the combat groups to take up their position, he left with his group towards the center of the village in order to destroy the German communication center connecting Cherbourg. The village was taken without any problems, with some thirty Germans captured and eleven killed whilst attempting to escape.

At 05h00, Krause sent a messenger to the regiment commander, Colonel William Ekman, with the message: « *I am in Sainte-Mère-Eglise!* ». An hour later, a second agent was sent with a new message: « *I have taken Sainte-Mère-Eglise!* ». But neither of the two messengers located Ekman. However, the second messenger did find General Ridgway and passed him the message. That morning, there were many messages which did not reach their recipients due to transmission problems. As a result of this, Colonel Ekman, by then less than one mile from the village, still believed until midday that Sainte-Mère-Eglise remained in the hands of the Germans.

The 2nd Battalion, commanded by Colonel Vandervoort, consisted of 575 out its original 630 paratroopers. At 06h15, when Vandervoort finally managed to make radio contact with Ekman, he informed him that he was in position at Neuville-Au-Plain. For nearly two hours, he was to have no news. At 08h00 he received orders, counter-orders and counter counter-orders characteristic of an operation behind enemy lines. Ekman first of all informed him that he had no news from Krause's 3rd Battalion. Then at 08h10, he ordered him to turn back and take Sainte-Mère-Eglise; then at 08h16 to return to Neuville, adding that the 3rd Battalion must at that moment be in Sainte-Mère-Eglise. At 08h17, he asked him to

La Fière bridge before the war. Its long roadway crossing the marshes was to be the theater of furious fighting between the Americans of the *82nd Airborne Division*, from the eastern bank, and the Germans counter-attacking in vain from the western bank. (Coll. D. François.)

Infantry from the *325th* inspecting a destroyed Renault tank on the La Fière roadway. (Ph. Marty Morgan.)

Pathfinders

In January 1944, a contingent of Pathfinders started its training, in preparation for Operation Neptune. The 82nd and 101st Airborne Divisions sent 300 of their paratroopers to the IX Troop Carrier Command Pathfinder School. Although some were volunteers, for many it was an assignment or even a disciplinary transfer. At the time, the Pathfinders did not have the mythical reputation they enjoy today.

In May, the Pathfinders force comprised 18 teams, three for each jump zone (there were 6 jump zones with code letters A, N, C, O, D and T). Each team, commanded by a lieutenant, consisted of 4 operators for two Eureka beacons and 4 men to provide a security perimeter around the operators. Each divisionary team (i.e. 3 teams) was commanded by a captain.

The equipment consisted of the Eureka beacon (AN/PPN-1A) carried by a paratrooper in a waterproof bag. The beacon had 5 reception frequencies and 5 transmission frequencies. The Rebecca receiver was installed in the cockpit of the C-47s. The plan was to send a Morse code message from the ground units to the pilots. For Operation Neptune, the letter of the drop zone assigned was sent continuously.

Visual signals were also planned, using « Holophane » lamps of different colors which would be used to mark out the drop zone (green lamp for drop zone « A » and « N », red for drop zones « C » and « O », amber for drop zones « D » and « T »).

1. Two infantrymen from the 325th posing in front of one of the three Renault tanks destroyed during the Battle of La Fière. (Ph. 82nd Airborne/D. François.)

2. La Fière roadway after the fighting on June 9 where the 325th GIR and 507th PIR were in action. The three Renault tanks were destroyed by Pvt. Marcus Heim from the 505th PIR. (Ph. D. François.)

3. In July at La Haye du Puits, General Omar Bradley awards the DSC to Lt. Col. Krause (505), Lt. Col. Vandervoort (505), Captain Rae (507), two Medic and Marcus Heim (505). (Ph. NA/D. François.)

Above : a number of destroyed vehicles after the fighting at La Fière. (Ph. D. François.)

Opposite : Marcus Heim, *505th PIR*. (Ph. D. François.)

A number of destroyed vehicles after the fighting at La Fière. (Ph. D. François.)

Above : Captain Robert Rae, from the 507th PIR, hero of the Battle of La Fière. (Ph. D. François.)

Opposite : La Fière manor after the fighting on June 9. (Ph. D. François.)

General Omar Bradley awards the *Distinguished Service Cross* to Marcus Heim for his bravery during the fighting at La Fière. (Ph. D. François.)

ignore the previous order and to go to Sainte-Mère-Eglise! Vandervoort, cautious after this stream of contradictions (remember that he was moving with a broken leg) decided to turn back, but to leave a group of forty paratroopers under the orders of Lt. Turner Turnbull of Co « C », to organize a skeleton defense of Neuville-Au-Plain.

At around 09h30, two companies of Georgians, supported by three light tanks and two self-propelled guns, attacked the 3rd Battalion to the south of Sainte-Mère-Eglise. These were repulsed by the men of the 3rd Battalion. Vandervoort now arrived with his 2nd Battalion. After discussion with Krause, the new arrivals were designated to ensure the defense to the north of the area.

During this time, Turnbull's group, running to reach their objective quickly, took Neuville in a few minutes. The village was unoccupied and Turnbull took up a position to the north of the commune on a promontory, overlooked by a hedgerow which provided him with a field of fire of over five hundred meters to the north. In an orchard bordered by uncovered terrain located to the west of Neuville, there was a group of ten men with a machine gun. To complete his disposition, Turnbull placed a bazooka gunner with two infantrymen in the houses bordering the RN 13 road.

Twenty minutes later, the men posted behind the hedge sighted a long column of German infantry singing on the road. At that moment Vandervoort arrived, now in a jeep delivered a few hours earlier by one of the gliders carrying the division's heavy equipment. Mounted on his jeep was a 57 mm gun. While the gunners positioned themselves to reinforce the support point, Vandervoort and Turnbull were talking when a Frenchman arrived on a bicycle. He pointed to the road behind him. In the distance, the two officers could indeed see a body of men marching. The man stated that they were German prisoners, escorted by paratroopers. While it was true that Vandervoort could see some men in paratrooper uniforms waving orange triangles, the perfect order of the

column made him uneasy. When the column was less than 800 meters away, Vandervoort no longer had any doubts, and ordered a machine gunner to open fire. In a flash, the column dispersed on either side of the road and returned fire. The Frenchman, meanwhile, took his chance to disappear.

It was a company of the Grenadier-Regiment 1058 of the 91.Luftl-Division, consisting of 190 men. Fierce fighting was to continue until the early afternoon. Turnbull's men, still lying in ambush behind their hedgerow to the west, had located the Germans along the road, but the Germans were trying to attack them from the flanks.

Vandervoort sent a messenger to ask Turnbull: « How is it going? Do you need any help? » The messenger returned with an assurance from Turnbull that everything was fine: « *Everything is OK and under control, don't worry about me!* ». Vandervoort trusted the reputation of the « Chief » (Turnbull was « half-Cherokee », nicknamed the « Chief » by his men, who respected his qualities as a warrior).

Shortly after the start of the battle, a German self-propelled gun appeared from the north less than 500 meters away and opened fire. The second shot it fired killed the bazooka gunner in his position at the roadside. Its fifth shot narrowly missed the anti-tank gun, whose crew headed for the shelter of a house. A few minutes later, they returned to retrieve their piece and managed to knock out the enemy gun with two shots. A German assault gun then emerged, a Sturmgeschütz, which they were lucky enough to damage.

Under the cover of the bocage, the German infantry tried to outflank Turnbull's positions, with the support of lethal mortar fire. By mid-afternoon, eighteen Americans had been killed or injured.

On returning to his CP, Vandervoort was informed of the bad news and sent Lt. Theodore L. Peterson and his section of the Co « C » to cover Turnbull's retreat. Once Turnbull had reached the perimeter of the battalion and was safe, Peterson, as the rear guard, could then disengage with his section.

By holding his position to the north of Neuville-Au-Plain throughout the whole day, Lt. Turner Turnbull stopped the progress of the Grenadier Regiment 1058 and protected the northern flank of the 82nd Airborne Division's forces, but at a cost of 25 men killed and injured out of the 41 paratroopers of his section. Turnbull himself was to be killed the following day by a mortar shell.

Drop Zone « T »

The sticks of the *507th PIR* were widespread on arrival at drop zone « T », located close to Amfreville. Only two of them touched down in the DZ, with enormous dispersion, covering a sector approximately 30 miles (50 km) (from Négreville to Graignes) by 12 miles (20 km). The 507th was to be the most widespread regiment of Operation Neptune. Its mission was to block the approaches to the west of the river Merderet, something which seemed impossible in the early hours of June 6. While most of the paratroopers were wading through flooded areas, the commander of the regiment, Colonel George Millett, gathered 40 paratroopers together and was trying to take Amfreville mid-morning. Failing in its attempt, the small group was forced to retreat to a position to the south-east of Laudes. Colonel Millet and part of the group were taken prisoner the following day.

Meanwhile, Lt. Col. Edwin Ostberg, commander of the 1st Battalion, who jumped with General Gavin, marched with 150 paratroopers of the 507th and 508th towards Cauquigny. Gavin decided to set up a first CP on the heights of La Fière and sent Ostberg towards the Chef du Pont bridge. Along the way, Ostberg met up with Captain Roy Creek who, after two tough battles, took the Chef du Pont bridge. Ostberg was wounded during this battle.

As for Lt. Col. Charles Timmes, commander of the 2nd Battalion, he had landed in a flooded area and gathered together a large group of scattered paratroopers, including gliders from the Detroit mission. At dawn, he reached Cauquigny, at the end of the La Fière roadway. He knew that this position was important but on hearing that morning the noise of the battle being fought at Amfreville, he decided to leave his position to support the elements fighting around the village, believing it to involve the main body of his battalion. His attempt also failed. The group pulled back in the direction of Cauquigny and set up in an apple orchard which would later become famous as the Timmes' Orchard.

Graignes

On June 6, 1944, the village of Graignes was the scene of a fierce battle fought between the elite of the German and American armies.

When the 82nd and 101st Airborne Divisions were dropped to the north of Carentan, the small village of Graignes, lost in its swamps some 6 miles (10 km) to the south, seemed to be far from the battle!

The HQ company of the 3rd Battalion, consisting mainly of the battalion's general staff, landed in the swampy waters of a calm sector.

Some of the paratroopers were drowned, tangled up in the shrouds of their parachutes and too heavily laden with equipment to be able to swim.

The survivors, helped by the light of the moon, advanced towards a 12th century church, jutting up into the sky at the top of a small hill. Latecomers continued arriving in the sector from all areas. Approximately 180 paratroopers gathered around Graignes under the command of Major Johnson, who decided to hold the village and to organize a defense point. Captain Leroy Brummit, Lieutenant Frank Naughton and Private Carlos Hurtado were among these survivors.

As the group was growing, the actions began. Defenses were dug, security posts set up and patrols sent to locate the enemy. The only bridge at the eastern entrance to the village was mined. A meeting was held by the mayor of the village, in which it was decided that the paratroopers would be given moral and logistics support. Villagers found equipment, supplies and munitions in the swamps, and supplied food and water for the soldiers. They also informed the Americans of the enemy activities and positions.

During the period from June 6 to 11, the Germans tested out the American defenses. On June 10, the paratroopers destroyed the bridge while a German patrol was preparing to cross it.

On Sunday June 11, while everyone was gathered in the old Roman church for the 11 a.m. mass, the Germans launched heavy artillery fire on the church and the American positions.

This was followed by a German assault, mainly consisting of SS from the 17th SS-Panzer-Grenadier Division "Götz von Berlichingen".

The paratroopers continued fighting whilst retreating. Private Carlos Hurtado was part of the group, armed only with light weapons, mortars and grenades. The fire exchanged with the Germans was so intense that, at around midnight, there was no ammunition left.

Once the Germans penetrated the American defensive perimeter, an organized retreat was no longer possible!

Major Johnson was killed during the attack, so Captain Brummit took command and decided to retreat through the swamps towards Carentan.

Tragedy strikes...

Captain Sophian, doctor of the battalion, had organized a mobile medical unit in the church, full of injured people, and refused to abandon these people during the retreat.

During the final assault on the church, the Waffen SS rounded up the final defenders who surrendered, the injured and the civilians who wished to remain with the Americans.

Captain Sophian and the injured were summarily shot in a field outside the village, in Mesnil-Angot. The priest was to be killed later in the village.

A few miles away, meanwhile, the escapees retreated into the swamps. They could see the destroyed church still smoking, at the top of this bloody hill. The village had become a martyr.

Drop Zone « N »

For the *508th PIR*, the drop was hardly any better than that of the 507th, with only eight sticks landing in the drop zone located to the north of Picauville. The regiment commander, Colonel Roy Lindquist, landed in the swamps of Amfreville (very close to Gavin). Many of the paratroopers of the 508th landed in other drop zones or in sectors solidly defended by the enemy, to the south and to the east of Picauville. Some even landed on the Normandy coast in the sector of the 101st Airborne.

One of the memorable events of the combats of the 508th was the attack by a small group of paratroopers from the 508th, led by Lt. Malcolm Brannen, on the command car of the German General W. Falley, commander of the 91st Infantry Division, close to his HQ in Bernaville. Falley and his aide were killed during this clash, returning early from a Kriegspiel in Rennes. His death, which his general staff only found out about 48 hours later, caused great confusion among the enemy, who were slow to react.

The largest force capable of regrouping was led by Lt. Col. Thomas Shanley on Hill 30 at Picauville. Shanley had with him some 200 paratroopers who he positioned around the hill. On several occasions, Shanley and his men fought off German assaults in the villages of Caponnet and Port Filiolet, assaults which never managed to penetrate the perimeter.

Landing Zone « O »

For the troops brought in on gliders, the Detroit mission started at dawn with the arrival of 52 Waco CG-4A gliders from the 436th Troop Carrier Group. The Waco were used in preference to the heavy English Horsa gliders when the mission was delayed by a few hours for a daytime landing. Detroit took two batteries of the 80th AAA/AT (anti-air defense) with various staff from the Signal Corps, 220 infantry, 16 guns and jeeps. During this mission, 23 gliders managed to land on or close to LZ « O », located at Forges.

The *325th GIR* arrived at around 07h00, landing about 2500 yards to the south-east of Sainte-Mère-Eglise. Many gliders were damaged on landing. The units were quickly assembled, however, and at around 10h15 all the battalions were ready. The 3rd Battalion headed in the direction of Carquebut, arriving at around 14h15 and reaching the area known as Le Port without encountering any opposition. The rest of the regiment went to an assembly area near Chef-du-Pont. At 16h00 Lt. Col. John Swenson received the order to send his unit to the east of La Fière to join the 505th. At the end of the day, 85 % of the members of the regiment were regrouped.

That evening, the Elmira mission got underway with the arrival of 22 Waco and 54 Horsa for the first echelon, then a further 14 Waco and 86 Horsa, making a total of 116 gliders. Starting at 21h00, the formation supplied the 82nd with an anti-tank battery plus personnel from the headquarters, a total of 437 men, 64 jeeps, 13 guns, etc.

Ridgway had decided that the original LZ "W" was too "risky" to be used, so DZ "O" was chosen for this operation.

Utah Beach

The Seaborne section of the 82nd, commanded by Colonel Edson Raff, landed at Utah Beach with the units of the 4th Infantry Division. Among his group was Co "F" of the 325th GIR (401st), Co "C" of the 746th Tank Battalion (attached to the division for Operation Neptune) and a section of the 4th Cavalry Recon Squadron. Raff reached Forges at top speed with his various units. The crossroads was the first objective before the capture of Sainte-Mère-Eglise.

To secure the LZ, Raff led an attack on Hill 20 and lost three Sherman tanks.

On the morning of June 7, things were not looking good for the division. From his command post at Sainte-Mère-Eglise, Ridgway could only produce a somewhat pessimistic report of the situation. His paratroopers were widely dispersed, numerous battalions had not assembled even half of their members, and there was no news from some of the battalion commanders. The bridges over the river Merderet were not yet in their hands and the advance of the 4th ID, which had managed to land and clear the beaches, had stopped in several places.

On the morning of June 7, an assault battalion of the 7th German army and the 2nd Battalion of the Gren.-Rgt. 1058, accompanied by Panzerjäger and an artillery support, attacked Sainte-Mère-Eglise to the west and the east. The German assault battalion, with some ten self-propelled guns, penetrated the lines of Co "D" of the 505th. Less than 50 meters from the CP of the 2nd Battalion, two German guns were destroyed by an American anti-tank gun. By chance, Raff's armored elements arrived from Forges and attacked the flanks of the enemy, causing them to retreat towards Neuville-Au-Plain.

Sainte-Mère-Eglise was finally liberated

June 9 : The Battle of La Fière

Although the bridge of La Fière was in American hands, Cauquigny was still not secured and the enemy seemed to be strengthening its positions there with infantry and 88 mm guns. The roadway was uncovered terrain under fire from the enemy, who were well established there. Any group wanting to lead an assault was exposed to hellish gunfire and faced considerable losses.

Ridgway decided to force a way through, since the bridge was of vital importance for the troops arriving from the beaches and waiting to the east.

Gavin ordered the Gliders of the 325th, whose numbers were still relatively intact, to attack the roadway up to the Cauquigny Chapel. The start point for the assault was in the courtyard of the La Fière farm, where a breach in the wall, caused by a shell, was to be the gateway to hell.

At 10h30, an artillery barrage triggered the start of the operation, followed by the 325th infantry assault. The Gliders crossed the wall and ran towards their fate. Many were killed a few meters after crossing the wall, while the most advanced rushed back into the trenches. The attack was broken.

Gavin decided to repeat the attack supported by the *507th PIR* led by a young officer, Captain Robert Rae. With 90 paratroopers, Rae got up and simply yelled: Let's go ! Charging forward with his men, they ran over the bodies strewn across the roadway. In spite of everything, the group made progress and arrived at Cauquigny. The 325th took over and pressed towards Amfreville. On the German side, the losses were enormous.

For his courage in this attack, in July 1944 Captain Robert Rae received the Distinguished Service Cross from General Bradley.

The road towards the center of Cotentin was opened.

The 508th, meanwhile, occupied Chef-du-Pont and was able to clear Hill 30, where Colonel Shanley was located.

In the following days, the 82nd fought at Saint-Sauveur-Le-Vicomte. Lt. Col. Vandervoort and his battalion entered the town after fierce fighting.

On June 17, the Cotentin was cut off and the return towards Cherbourg was possible.

The battle in the hills of La Haye-du-Puits

In order to carry out Operation Cobra, led by General George Patton and the armored vehicles of his 3rd Army, which needed to break through towards the south of the department, La Haye-du-Puits had to be taken. But above all the heights dominating the town had to be taken, to open up a route for Patton's breakthrough.

For this operation, the 82nd was again called into action. The Division was to fight until the early days of July, with the worst fighting on July 4, America's national day of celebration.

The most violent combat took place on Hills 131 and 95 in the sector of Blanche Lande Abbey and La Poterie. The enemy was firmly entrenched on the high ground, with 88 mm guns, machine gun and mortar nests. The taking of this high ground was to prove very costly.

After 33 days fighting, the « All American » was finally relieved on July 8, 1944. The cost of the campaign had been enormous - of the 12,000 men involved, 5245 were killed or injured, a total of 46 % losses (1282 killed in action and 2373 seriously wounded).

After returning to England the Division quickly resumed training, in preparation for a new mission.

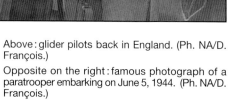

Above : glider pilots back in England. (Ph. NA/D. François.)

Opposite on the right : famous photograph of a paratrooper embarking on June 5, 1944. (Ph. NA/D. François.)

Above : jump jacket of General James Gavin displayed at West Point Museum. (Ph. D. François.)

Opposite : gliders flying at dawn over Utah Beach. (Ph. NA/D. François.)

Above : a stick from the *508th PIR*. (Ph. D. François.)

Below : Rennes hospital, where the injured POW paratroopers are transferred. On this photograph, Major Gordon Smith (507) with two officers from the *101st Airborne Division*. (Ph. D. François.)

168

5. A paratrooper talking with children at Ravenoville. (Ph. NA/D. François.)

6. Saint Marcouf. (Ph. NA/D. François.)

7. Saint Marcouf. (Ph. NA/D. François.)

8. Saint Marcouf. (Ph. NA/D. François.)

1. Bulldozer leaving a Waco glider. (Ph. NA/D. François.)

2. The bodies of the paratroopers are identified before being buried in provisional cemeteries. (Ph. NA/D. François.)

3. A paratrooper has found a friend after the battle. (Ph. NA/D. François.)

4. Saint Marcouf village : arrival of paratroopers from the 82nd. (Ph. D. François.)

A combat team, armed with a machine gun, going past a horse-drawn wagon abandoned in the Saint-Marcouf sector (NA.)

Wary, paratroopers from the *508th PIR* lost in the Saint-Marcouf sector question civilians. The lieutenant we see here seems to be dubious. (NA.)

Above : Aid Station of the *82nd* at Etienville. (Ph. NA/D. François.)

Opposite : a soldier from the *325th GIR* has a radio contact, in a garden at Etienville. (Ph. NA/D. François.)

Near the Saint-Marcouf church, a group of lost paratroopers from the *508th PIR* asking an old lady for information. (Ph. NA.)

Surprised civilians watch as these soldiers from a glider regiment go past. (Ph. NA.)

British made Horsa gliders. The Americans also used the Airspeed Horsa A5 51, since it could carry far more men and equipment (including jeeps and howitzers) than the Waco. The above photograph shows the two ramps used to disembark a Jeep which had been carried by this Horsa. (Ph. NA/D. François.)

The difficult terrain in the Cotentin region, broken by numerous hedges, seriously damaged many gliders on landing. *Brigadier General* Don Pratt was to die in one of these accidents. On this photograph, bodies lined up near the wreck of a Horsa glider. (NA.)

Wehrmacht soldiers killed in the Ham sector. (Ph. NA/D. François.)

Aid Station in the Sainte-Mère-Eglise sector. (Ph. NA/D. François.)

Units from the *82nd Airborne Division* landing at Utah Beach. (Ph. NA/D. François.)

264 B. - Arrond^t de Valognes. - Château de Bernaville à Picauville

1. Bernaville Castle, before the war, headquarters of General Wilhem Falley. (Coll. D. François.)

2. A paratrooper from the 508th has just found enough food to last several days. (Ph. D. François.)

3. C-47 destroyed in the marshes at Isle Marie, Picauville. (Ph. D. François.)

4. Captain Paul Smith (507) awarded the rank of Major by Colonel Edson Raff. (Ph. D. François.)

5. *Major Gordon Smith* (507th PIR). (Ph. D. François.)

6. Sgt. Carl Letson from the *507th PIR*, he landed at Négreville and was to be taken prisoner. (Ph. D. François.)

1

SAINTE-MÈRE-ÉGLISE (Manche) – La Fête-Dieu

2

3

Sainte-Mère Eglise (Manche) – Route de Carentan

Vve Bigard, Mercerie.
F. Féron, éditeur, Caen.

4

1. Sainte-Mère-Eglise before the war

2. Lt. Col. Ekmann from the *505th PIR*. (Ph. 82nd ABN/D. François.)

3. Sainte-Mère-Eglise before the war

4. Formations of C-47s and gliders arriving over Normandy.(Ph. D. François.)

5. Lt. Gene Williams, Pathfinder, he was to be killed at Prétot on June 20. (Ph. D. François.)

6. Sainte-Mère-Eglise before the war. Compare this photograph with the one at the bottom of page 186, taken at the same place in June 1944.

SAINTE-MÈRE-ÉGLISE (Manche) — Rue de la Mer

Above : the gliders tried to clear a landing zone through the bocage hedgerows. (Ph. NA/D. François.)

LA NORMANDIE — « La C. P. A

9. Environs de SAINTE-MÈRE-ÉGLISE — FAUVILLE — Le Vieux Château

Opposite : Fauville Castle, German headquarters at Sainte-Mère-Eglise.

50. - Ste-MÈRE-ÉGLISE (Manche). - Rue de Carentan

Sainte-Mère-Eglise before the war.

Officers from the *505th PIR*, Ekmann and Krause are in the center. (Ph. 82nd ABN/D. François.)

Two paratroopers from the 508th watching the sector from the edge of a field. (Ph. D. François.)

Container drop in the days after D-Day. (Ph. D. François.)

182

One of the first paratroopers killed on June 6, 1944. (Ph. D. François.)

The first paratroopers enter Sainte Mère Eglise. They used horses from the nearby farms. (Ph. NA/D. François.)

Lieutenant-colonel Benjamin Vandervoort from the *505th PIR*. (Ph. 82nd ABN/D. François.)

Paratroopers on horseback entering Sainte-Mère-Eglise, June 6. Photograph taken at the same place as the one shown on the top of 181. (Ph. NA/D. François.)

The paratroopers now hold Sainte-Mère-Eglise, a strategic crossroads for the troops coming from the beaches. (Ph. NA/D. François.)

After the fighting, civilians from Sainte-Mère-Eglise come out of their shelters and find paratroopers from the 82nd in their village. (Ph. NA/D. François.)

Captain Robert Piper from the *505th PIR* next to a British Horsa glider. (Ph. 82nd ABN/D. François.)

The chaplain from the *505th PIR*, "Chappie" Wood. (Ph. 82nd ABN/D. François.)

Carlson Smith and his friend Dub Murray, both from the 507th. Dud was to be killed at Graignes. (Ph. D. François.)

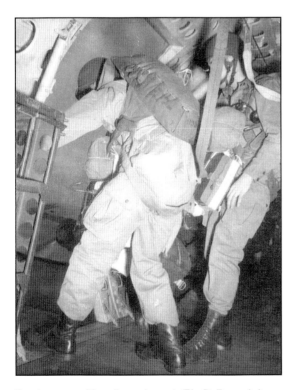

Paratroopers with radio equipment. (Ph. D. François.)

Paratroopers from the 508th resting on Norman soil. (Ph. D. François.)

Corporal Walther Choquette from the 507th. He was to be killed at Graignes on June 10. (Ph. D. François.)

185

Paratroopers from the 508th having a moment's break in the shelter of a hedge. (Ph. D. François.)

Sainte-Mère-Eglise was damaged by the infantry fighting, at the crossroads north of the square, looking down Cap de Laine street. Compare with the photograph on page 179. (Ph. NA/D. François.)

1. A paratrooper from the 505th has recovered a German horse, south of Sainte-Mère-Eglise. (Ph. NA/D. François.)

2. A doctor from the 505th examining an injured soldier in the Sainte-Mère-Eglise sector. (Ph. NA/D. François.)

3. Ceremony at the provisional cemetery, Sainte-Mère-Eglise. (Ph. NA/D. François.)

4. A paratrooper chaplain blessing the bodies of paratroopers killed during the Battle of Normandy. (Ph. NA/D. François.)

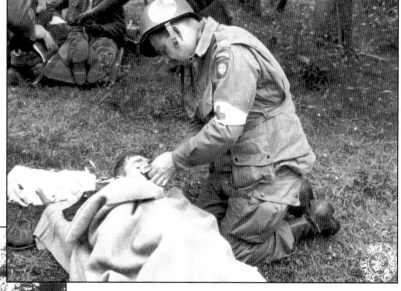

Lt. Frank Naughton, during the Battle of the Ardennes. In Normandy, he fought in the Graignes sector. (Ph. D. François.)

Captain David Brummit from the *507th PIR*. He was to land on Norman soil in Graignes marshes. (Ph. D. François.)

Graignes village, after the battle. (Ph. D. François.)

French vehicle reused by the Germans and destroyed in the Neuville au Plain sector. (Ph. D. François.)

1 and 2. Sainte-Mère-Eglise before the war.

— SAINTE-MÈRE-ÉGLISE (Manche). — Rue de la Gare. E. F.

A. Mouchel, Sainte-Mère-Eglise.

1

10. Sainte-Mère-Eglise (Manche). — Rue de la Gare

2

189

Sainte-Mère-Eglise before the war.

Sainte-Mère-Église — L'Église

Edition Mme Fortin, Sainte-Mère-Église

An officer from the *508th* finds a moment's respite near a wall. (Ph. D. François.)

Colonel Louis Mendez, a West-Pointer, commanding the 3rd Battalion of the *508th* in Normandy. (Ph. D. François.)

Robert White from the *508th PIR.* (Ph. D. François.)

Lt. Lester W. Pollom from the *508th PIR.* (Ph. D. François.)

Pvt. George Strenkle from the *508th PIR.* (Ph. D. François.)

Ed Rokosz from the *508th PIR.* (Ph. D. François.)

Lt. Bodack, taken prisoner in Normandy, wounded during his transfer to Rennes by the American aviation. He was to survive the war, hemiplegic. (Ph. D. François.)

Jack Schlegel, in 1945, wearing an Ike jacket with the British jump wings. During the Normandy campaign, he was to be taken prisoner at Picauville, then transferred to Rennes. He managed to escape in August and get back to the American lines near Avranches. (Ph. D. François.)

Group of soldiers from the 508th who had been taken prisoner and managed to escape. Jack Schlegel is in the first row. (Ph. D. François.)

Jack Schlegel, then a young paratrooper at Fort Benning. (Ph. D. François.)

The Renaud family at Sainte-Mère-Eglise together with some paratroopers. (Ph. NA/D.François.)

Many gliders were to be damaged in the Normandy bocage countryside. (Ph. D. François.)

LA BASSE-NORMANDIE PITTORESQUE
3101. - Ste-MÈRE-ÉGLISE (Manche). - L'Église
(Au premier plan Vieille Croix très curieuse)

Coll. Mouchel, Ste-Mère-Eglise

Cliché A. V.

L. G. B., Saint-Pier

George Strenkle (see p. 191) on June 5, 1944 in England. (Ph. D. François.)

Sainte-Mère-Eglise church before the war.

Paratroopers from the *508th PIR* in a Norman field. (Ph. D. François.)

A paratrooper from the *82nd* observing the terrain. (Ph. D. François.)

A short break for these paratroopers from the 82nd. (Ph. D. François.)

A civilian in the destroyed village of Picauville. (Ph. D. François.)

The top end of Picauville village has been severely damaged during the fighting. (Ph. D. François.)

Two paratroopers from the 82nd resting in a shelter. (Ph. D. François.)

The first jeeps of the 82nd cross Picauville. (Ph. D. François.)

General James Gavin. (Ph. NA/D. François.)

James McCallum from the *505th PIR*. He participated in the four jumps made by his regiment, in Sicily, Italy, Normandy and Holland. (Ph. D. François.)

OB. Hill from the 508th PIR, he landed in the Beuzeville au Plain marshes. (Ph. D. François.)

Soldiers (see page 196) from the *508th PIR*, OB. Hill is the second on the right. (Ph. D. François.)

Reinforced M.1942 jump jacket which belonged to a paratrooper from the *505th PIR*. (Coll. D.DAy Museum.)

A Waco glider has just landed on the roof of a garage at Sebbeville, its pilot is in the foreground. (Ph. D. François.)

1. Colonel Roy Lindquist, commanding the *508th PIR* in Normandy. (Ph. D. François.)

2. A Horsa glider has landed safely on the LZ south of Sainte-Mère-Eglise. (Ph. D. François.)

3. A jeep, transported by glider, is used to carry wounded soldiers. Medical units have been set up in barns or under a parachute shelter. (Ph. 82nd Airborne/D. François.)

4. Paratroopers taken prisoner crossing Valognes. This photograph was taken secretly by an inhabitant of Valognes. (Ph. D. François.)

Men from the *325th GIR* setting up a mortar, an efficient weapon in hedge warfare. (Ph. 82nd Airborne/D. François.)

Officers from the *325th GIR* examining a map. Colonel Lewis, commanding the *325th*, is on the left. (Ph. 82nd Airborne/D. François.)

Tanks of the *746 Tank Battalion* arrive to support the paratroopers from the 82nd. (Ph. D. François.)

A strongpoint of the 325th, a .30-caliber machine gun is ready for action. (Ph. 82nd Airborne/D. François.)

A soldier from the *325th GIR*. (Ph. 82nd Airborne/D. François.)

1. Airborne troops from the *325th* with an 81 mm mortar. (Ph. 82nd Airborne/D. François.)

2. American armband. (Coll. D. François)

3. German assault gun destroyed by the *505th PIR* at the entrance of Sainte-Mère-Eglise. (Ph. 82nd Airborne/D. François.)

1. Young girl watching the paratroopers from the *82nd Airborne Division,* in admiration. (D. François.)

2 and **3.** Paratroopers from the *507th PIR* check the houses in a village. (D. François.)

4 and **5.** Villagers welcoming the liberators. (Ph. D. François.)

4. Infantrymen from the *325th GIR* on the road to Amfreville. (Ph. D. François.)

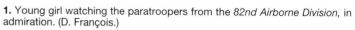

Two paratroopers from the 82nd, looking exhausted, take the time to pose for a photograph in the Picauville sector. (Ph. D. François.)

These two paratroopers from the *508th PIR*, one armed with a USM1-A1 carbine, take a short break before returning to the fight in the Picauville sector. (Ph. D. François.)

1. General Wilhem Falley, Commanding the 91st Infantry Division. He was to be killed on June 6 by Lt. Malcolm Brannen and his men, on the road from his Bernaville head-quarters to Picauville. (Coll. Charita/Heimdal.)

2. Paratroopers from the *505th PIR* advancing along a road in the Sainte-Mère-Eglise sector. (Ph. 82nd Airborne/D. François.)

3. A Waco glider has crashed, like many others, in a hedge of the bocage. (NA.)

Paratroopers from the *508th PIR* fighting in the bocage. (Ph. D. François.)

Temporary graves of General Wilhem Falley and his deputy, commander Joachim Bartuzat. (Ph. D. François.)

Lt. Col. Maloney from the *507th PIR*. (Ph. D. François.)

Lt. Gene Williams from the *508th PIR*.

Light vehicles of the 82nd cross villages destroyed during the fighting. (Ph. D. François.)

Picauville was severely damaged by the bombing. (Ph. D. François.)

Mortar sections from the *508th* set up batteries of 81 mm mortars. (Ph. D. François.)

A Horsa glider which landed on the Sebbeville LZ is going to be destroyed. Continued on the top of the page opposite. (Ph. D. François.)

Capitain George Simons from *508th PIR*, killed on July 4 on Hill 95. (Ph. D. François.)

1. The glider is going to destroyed. (Ph. D. François.)

2. A paratrooper from the *508th PIR* has dug a foxhole in the shelter of a hedge. (Ph. D. François.)

3. A paratrooper from the *508th PIR* has just received his wing, in a few months time he will fight on Hill 30 in Normandy. (Ph. D. François.)

4. A group of paratroopers from the 82nd and 101st Airborne Divisions have landed in the Val de Saire, more than 12 miles (20 kilometers) from their DZ. After surviving a few days behind enemy lines, they were to be taken prisoner in Videscoville woods. (Ph. from private archives.)

1. Two paratroopers from the *508th* ready to board. (Ph. D. François.)

2. A paratrooper from the 82nd, name unknown, was injured in the bocage. (Ph. D. François.)

3. A paratrooper from the *508th* armed with an USM1-A1 has set up his firing position by a hedge in the Chef du Pont sector. (Ph. D. François.)

4. Two paratroopers from the 82nd, worn out by the fighting, have dropped exhausted into a ditch. (Ph. D. François.)

5. A paratrooper proudly showing the greatcoat of a German soldier. (Ph. D. François.)

6. Even when they are wounded, the paratroopers' morale remains high. (Ph. D. François.)

7. Two paratroopers resting in a ditch, one of them has a field dressing on his ankle. (Ph. D. François.)

The 325th in action at Ham. (Ph. D. François.)

Paratroopers from the 82nd advancing along the lanes at Picauville. (Ph. D. François.)

The Bon Sauveur hospital in Picauville, in ruins. (Ph. D. François.)

1. General Gavin talking with an officer from the 82nd. (Ph. D. François.)

2. General James Gavin, deputy commander of the 82nd Airborne Division. (Ph. D. François.)

3. Two officers from the 82nd trying to pinpoint their location on a map, difficult in such an unfamiliar environment. (Ph. D. François.)

4. Paratroopers on all the roads of the Sainte-Mère-Eglise canton conver-ging towards their objectives. (Ph. D. François.)

1. A German or Georgian prisoner is waiting in a ditch, a resigned look on his face. Photograph taken by Lt. Williams from the *508th*. (Ph. D. François.)

2. German assault gun from the Panzerjäger-Abteilung 709, still smoking in the morning of June 7; it was destroyed by private J. Atchley from the H/505. This photograph was taken a few hundred yards north of the village on the RN 13 road, north of Sainte-Mère-Eglise. (NA.)

3. From June 16, paratroopers from the *505th PIR* control Saint-Sauveur-Le-Vicomte. This famous photograph shows Lieutenant Colonel Benjamin Vandervoort (commanding the 2nd Battalion of the *505th PIR*) in the middle of the town in ruins, leaning on his crutch. In the background, we can see the road sign for La Haye-du-Puits, which would only be captured a month later. (NA.)

4. Dead American paratroopers wrapped in a parachute will be buried temporarily at Sainte-Mère-Eglise. (Ph. NA/D. François.)

5. German paratroopers killed by their American counterparts. German paratroopers from the 1st Battalion of the FJR6 (von der Heydte's regiment) encountered stiff resistance on the outskirts of Sainte-Marie-du-Mont; they were surrounded by American paratroopers (mainly from the *101st Airborne Division*) during the night of 6-7 June. These bodies were photographed in the Sainte-Mère-Eglise sector. (Ph. NA/D. François.)

Frank Naughton, then a young paratrooper. In Normandy, he was to land in the Graignes marshes and fight against the *Waffen-SS* of the *17th SS-Panzergrenadier-Division*. (Ph. D. François.)

Page opposite, top right: Sergeant Bill How from the 3rd Battalion, *508th PIR.* He became the bodyguard of Colonel Louis Mendez. (Ph. D. François.)

A paratrooper from the *508th PIR* in front of the graves of two German soldiers. (Ph. D. François.)

Above: a German soldier killed at the entrance of Pont-l'Abbé, in the commune of Picauville. Photograph taken by lieutenant Williams, commanding the *Pathfinders of the 508th*. (Ph. D. François.)

A paratrooper from the *508th PIR* resting in a ditch. (Ph. D. François.)

1. Civilians move the German bodies unceremoniously. (Ph. NA/D. François.)

2. This other photograph taken in Saint-Sauveur-le-Vicomte on June 16 is taken from the same place as the previous one (see page 214) but looking the other way, towards the west. Lieutenant Colonel Vandervoort continued to advance, leaning on his crutch, his jeep stayed in the middle of the street. (NA/D. François.)

3. Madame Dijon leaves the village of Sainte-Mère-Eglise, helped by paratroopers on June 12. The dramatic situation does not affect her legendary good spirits. (Ph. NA/D. François.)

4. A Medic from the *307th Airborne Medical Company* provides first aid to a wounded German soldier. (Ph. NA/D. François.)

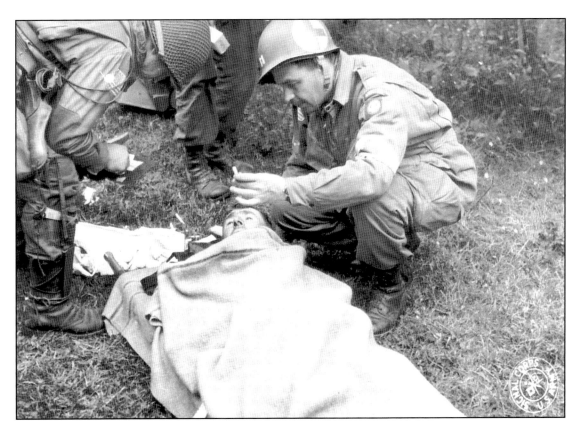

A paratrooper medic provides first aid to a German prisoner. (Ph. NA/D. François.)

A German vehicle destroyed by the paratroopers from the 82nd in Saint-Sauveur-le-Vicomte sector. (Ph. NA/D. François.)

Two paratroopers rejoin their unit after spending several days behind enemy lines. (Ph. NA/D. François.)

South entry of Sainte-Mère-Eglise. (Ph. D. François.)

Men from the 325th have requisitioned a German Kettenkrad. (Ph. D. François.)

Lieutenant Briand Beaudin (on the left) Doctor from the 3rd Battalion of the *508th PIR* and Lt. Paul E. Lehman from the same battalion, at Orglandes on June 17, 1944. (Ph. 82nd Airborne/D. François.)

Patch of the *82nd Airborne Division*. (Coll. D. François.)

Picauville is in ruins. (Ph. D. François.)

Lt. Gene H. Williams, commanding a team of Pathfinders from the 508th. He was to be killed on June 20 while liberating the village of Prétot. (Ph. D. François.)

Lt. Malcolm Brannen, officier du *508th PIR*. (Ph. D. François.)

After the Battle of Normandy, General James Gavin meets the regiments of the 82nd. This photograph shows the *507th PIR* commanded by Colonel Raff who has replaced Colonel Millett (POW). (Ph. D. François.)

Above: Lt. Col. Mendez with his driver. He was to take command of the 508th at the end of the war. (Ph. D. François.)

Opposite: *Major* Tom Shanley, during the Battle of Normandy. He was to hold Hill 30 with his battalion, tying down a large enemy force. (Ph. D. François.)

This paratrooper who arrived by glider was probably killed when leaving the glider. His body seems to have been searched. (Ph. D. François.)

1. On the road to Baupte, a section of German cyclists has been killed by the men of Company D from the 508th. (Ph. D. François.)

2. A C-47 carrying paratroopers crashed in the marsh opposite Ile Marie castle at Picauville. (Ph. D. François.)

3. Robert White from the 508th examining a German soldier he had killed as the German was shooting at him. We can see the mark of a bullet on his right sleeve. (Ph. D. François.).

Above : two *Medics* from the 507th taking a break after the battle of La Fière. (Ph. D. François.)

Below : Graignes church after the fighting: the wounded paratroopers left in the church were to be executed at Mesnil Angot by the SS. (Ph. D. François.)

1. *Sgt.* Frank Staples on the left. (Ph. D. François.)

2. Captain Chet Graham from the 508th, he has just recovered a German motorcycle on Hill 30. (Ph. D. François.)

3. Irwin Shanley from the *508th PIR*, fighting alongside Major Shanley (unrelated) on Hill 30 at Picauville. (Ph. D. François.)

4. Two paratroopers from the 82nd take a short break before returning to the assault on Hill 95. (Ph. D. François.)

A paratrooper in the Normandy bocage. (Ph. D. François.

Paratroopers from the 508th have set up their bivouac in this ditch. (Ph. D. François.)

Henri Joseph Hirleman, Co «I» from the 325th GIR, a *Pathfinder* during Operation *Market Garden*. (Ph. D. François.)

S.R. Hartline from the *325th GIR*. (Ph. D. François.)

Infantrymen from the 325th firing a mortar to dislodge the enemy firmly positioned in the hedges. (Ph. 82nd Airborne/D. François.)

Men from the 325th provide covering fire with a water-cooled Browning machine gun. (Ph. 82nd Airborne/D. François.)

Opposite : an infantryman from the 325th, armed with a
Garand rifle, discovers hedge fighting. (Ph. 82nd Airbor-
ne/D. François.)

Captain Roy Creek from the *507th PIR* and his men liberate Chef du Pont. (Ph. D. François.)

Pvt. Ed Jewziorski from the *507th PIR,* he was to fight at La Fière and take part in Captain Rae's famous assault. (Ph. D. François.)

Two paratroopers from the *507th PIR,* on the right Sgt. Giacoletti. (Ph. D. François.)

Two *Medics* taking a break after the fierce fighting at La Fière. (Ph. D. François.)

Lt. Chris Heisler from the *507th PIR*, he landed at Négreville and was to be taken prisoner the next day. (Ph. D. François.)

Sgt. George Leidenheimer from the *507th PIR*, captured on June 6, he escaped from Valognes and rejoined the American lines a few days later. (Ph. D. François.)

Pvt. Jack Summers from the *507th PIR*. (Ph. D. François.)

Pvt. Joe Lizut from the *508th PIR*. (Ph. D. François.)

1. Captain Morgan Bra-konecke from the *507th PIR*. (Ph. D. François.)

2. *Pvt.* Lou Horn from the 507, he was to fight at Chef du Pont and La Fière. (Ph. D. François.)

3. John Hinchliff from the *507th PIR*, machine gunner, he fought right till the end in Graignes village. (Ph. D. François.)

4. *Cpl.* Howard Huebner from the *507th PIR*. (Ph. D. François.)

5. Captain Verret, cha-plain from the *507th PIR*. (Ph. D. François.)

6. Carl Letson back in the United States. (Ph. D. François.)

7. *Lt.* Frank Naughton is promoted to the rank of captain by Colonel Edson Raff after the Normandy Campaign. (Ph. D. François.)

8. Pvt. Gail Sauer from the *507th PIR.* (Ph. D. François.)

9. Captain Roy Creek is promoted to the rank of *Major* by Colonel Edson Raff. (Ph. D. François.)

1. Jack Summers from the 507th PIR. (Ph. D. François.)

2. Lt. Gaul from the 508ᵉ, he was to be taken prisoner in Normandy. (Ph. D. François.)

3. Cpl. Jack Schlegel back from Normandy, proudly displaying the standard of General Falley, found in the General's car. (Ph. D. François.)

Lt. Malcolm Brannen and his men, lay an ambush for General Falley. (Ph. D. François.)

Below : Lt. Colonel Louis Mendez (on the left), parachuted far from his drop zone, it was to take him several days before he would find his battalion. (Ph. D. François.)

Above : the soldiers wounded during the fierce fighting in Normandy, on the now open road to Utah Beach, from where they will set sail for England. (Ph. D. François.)

Below : men from Co « B » of the *507th PIR* after the Battle of Normandy. (Ph. D. François.)

Provisional grave in a temporary cemetery in Normandy. (Ph. NA/D. François.)

Two civilians laying flowers on the provisional grave of a paratrooper. (Ph. NA/D. François.)

Above and opposite: after the war, men from the *508th PIR* were to be decorated by General Gentilhomme at Sainte-Mère-Eglise. (Ph. D. François.)

237

A stick from the *82nd Airborne Division* before boarding. (Ph. 82nd Airborne.)

Holland

During the days following its return to England, the 82nd Division underwent important changes. *Major General* Matthew Ridgway left the division and took command of the recently formed 18th Airborne Corps, in August 1944. He was promoted *Lieutenant General* and command of the division was given to General Gavin who, at the same time, was made Major General.

Due to the proliferation of airborne units in the Allied Forces, on August 21, 1944 the *1st Allied Airborne Army* was created, commanded by *Lieutenant General* Lewis H. Brereton.

The *1st Allied A/B Army* consisted of the 18th A/B Corps and its thee airborne divisions, the 82nd, the 101st and the 17th, as well as the British 1st and 6th Airborne Divisions, the Polish 1st Independent Parachute Brigade and the US *9th Troop Carrier Command*.

The 82nd was also reorganized. The 507th rejoined the 17th Airborne Division and the final structure included the 504th, the 505th and the 508th and the 325th Glider Regiment.

Early September, General Montgomery devised a plan to seize the bridges over the rivers Maas, Waal and Rhine, opening the way for a thrust by the British 30th Corps to Arnhem. The 30th Corps then had to advance deep into the heart of Germany. The operation was codenamed *Market Garden*.

In the first phase of the operation, *Market*, three airborne divisions had to make a parachute drop into key sectors. The 101st would have to jump in the south, near the town of Eindhoven and then make contact with the British 30th Corps. The 82nd Airborne Division would then have to jump south of Nijmegen and take the bridges over the river Waal as well as Grave bridge. The third objective, located north of Arnhem, was assigned to the British 1st Airborne Division and the Polish 1st Independent Airborne Brigade.

Garden, the ground phase, was carried out by the units of the British 30th Corps preceded by the *Guards Armored Division*.

The operation was planned to start on September 17, 1944.

On the day, 1545 troop transport aircraft and 478 gliders took off from the 24 British airfields. The C-47 formations were escorted by 1130 fighters.

General Gavin would jump with the leading element, the 505th commanded by Colonel Ekman, followed by the *307th Airborne Engineer Battalion*, jumping as a unit formed for this operation. Paratroopers from Colonel Tucker's 504th would follow, then Lindquist's 508th and Colonel Griffith's *376th Parachute Field Artillery Battalion*.

The 82nd would have a total force of 7250 paratroopers on the ground.

The division was flown over the drop zone with the loss of only one aircraft. The paratroopers jumped onto drop zones identified by the letters O, N and T. The Pathfinders, led by Lt. Col. C. W. Jaubert, jumped onto DZ «O» near Overasselt at 12h47. The 505th landed on DZ «N» south of Groesbeck between 13h00 and 13h12. The 504th which followed landed on DZ «O» between 13h15 and 13h19. At 13h21, the first paratroopers from the Engineers Regiment landed near Groesbeck. Colonel Lindquist and his paratroopers from the 508th landed north of the town on DZ »T», between 13h26 and 13h31. The 376th Artillery Regiment was parachuted onto DZ «N» at 13h33.

The operation over Holland was the most accurate mass airborne mission in history.

Taking advantage of the element of surprise, the paratroopers reached their objectives and took the various bridges they had been assigned. Grave Bridge was taken by the 2nd Battalion of the 504th, two hours after landing. The 1st Battalion had to seize four other

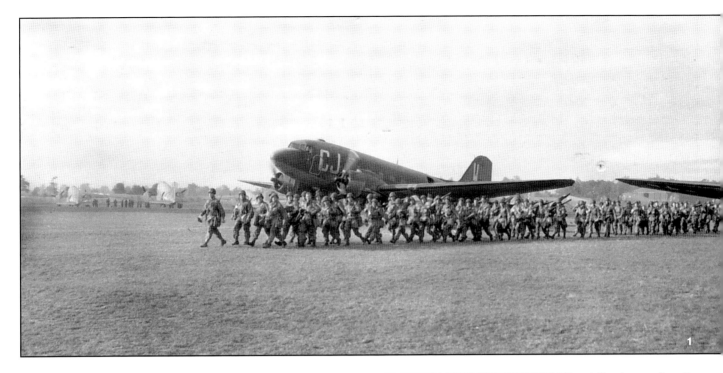

1. Paratroopers from the two US airborne divisions set out from various British airfields for Operation Market Garden. (Ph. NA/D. François.)

2 and 3. Two paratroopers from the *508th PIR* waiting calmly for the boarding order. (Ph. D. François.)

bridges over the Maas-Waal Canal. The most southerly bridge was captured by Co «B» and the paratroopers from the 505th. The 504th, 505th and 508th reached the two bridges near the villages of Malden and Hatert, just to see them blown up as they approached. The Germans had mined the bridges before retreating.

Due to superior enemy forces, the first attempts to take the Nijmegen bridges (road and rail) failed.

General Gavin ordered Lt. Col. Shields Warren and his battalion to take the road bridge as quickly as possible. With a Dutch guide, Companies «A» and «B» reached Nijmegen and found the post office where the firing mechanism for the explosives camouflaged under the bridge had been set up. The rest of the two companies was soon to be engaged against a large force of Germans, which prevented them from crossing the bridge for several days.

In the background, gliders are also waiting for the order to take off. (Ph. D. François.)

239

Above : General Gavin ready for Operation Market Garden. (Ph. 82nd Airborne.)

Opposite : a few hours before the start of Operation Market Garden, General James Gavin putting on his equipment before the big jump. (Ph. NA/D. François.)

A stick of paratroopers from the 82nd en route for Holland. (Ph. NA/D. François.)

In the morning of September 19, the first elements of the *Guards Armored Division* made contact with the 82nd in the Grave sector. With the Nijmegen road now cleared, the units of the 30th Corps were able to come to the rescue and take the bridge.

Less than one hour before the Gliders from the 82nd landed, a large enemy force attacked to the east of Groesbeck from Reichswald forest and surrounded the landing zones. Elements from the 505th and the 508th were soon engaged in desperate fighting to take the high ground in the sector. Luckily, the LZ was cleared just before the gliders landed. During this action, 1st Sergeant Leonard Funk from Co «C» of the 508th, led a small group of paratroopers and knocked out four 20 mm guns and three AA guns and killed 15 enemy soldiers. Funk was awarded the *Distinguished Service Cross* for his action.

Now that they had taken the bridge, the paratroopers from the 82nd were hoping to be relieved by the British tanks. Unfortunately, with no infantry support, the tanks were unable to advance as planned. This was an immense disappointment for the paratroopers, and a wasted sacrifice. As for the English paratroopers at Arnhem, they were never to be relieved. After holding out for four days, longer than planned, the 120 survivors from Colonel John Frost's 2nd Parachute Battalion were forced to surrender. Out of the 12,000 Polish and British paratroopers sent to take the «Bridge too far» at Arnhem, less than 2000 rejoined the lines. After evacuating the survivors from the Arnhem sector, the Allies moved from an offensive to a defensive position.

The Allies and the Dutch civilians suffered heavy casualties during Operation *Market Garden*. During the nine days of the operation, the Allies lost over 17,000 men (killed, wounded or missing in action). The 82nd Airborne Division alone lost 1432 men.

On November 11, 1944, British troops arrived to start relieving the 82nd, which could begin the transfers to the Suippes-Sissonne rest camp near Rheims in France.

The radio equipment is wrapped in a blanket, then packed in a container which will be released over the drop zone. (Ph. D. François.)

A Howitzer is being pushed into a Waco. (Ph. D. François.)

Parachute drops during the daytime are straightforward. (Ph. 82nd Airborne.)

241

Photographs page 243 :

1. The gliders landed during the day in the Holland plain. (Ph. D. François.)

2. Two glider pilots posing beside a modified Waco CG-4A. (Ph. D. François.)

3. Soldiers from the *325th GIR* examine a damaged Waco. (Ph. D. François.)

Jeeps are unloaded from the Wacos. (Ph. NA/D. François.)

A jeep has just been taken out of a Waco. (Ph. D. François.)

(GPR-131-2-HQ/XTCC)(3-FEB.45) OLD CANVAS SIDES

General James Gavin presents the officers of the 82nd Division to General Sir Miles Dempsey, commanding the Second British Army. (Ph. NA/D. François.)

General Gavin and *Lieutenant General* Browning, commanding the British airborne forces. (Ph. 82nd Airborne.)

General Gavin briefs his staff before the jump in Holland. (Ph. NA/D. François.)

General Gavin with his staff in a jeep brought by glider. (Ph. NA/D. François.)

Gavin and an officer from his staff in a wood in the Grave sector. (Ph. 82nd Airborne.)

General Gavin and General Miles Dempsey. Dempsey was to say that the 82nd was the best division in the Allies. (Ph. NA/D. François.)

General Gavin with officers from the *505th PIR*. (Ph. 82nd Airborne.)

Gavin meets the Britishparatroopers. (Ph. 82nd Airborne.)

The British armored vehicles from the « Garden » phase of the operation. (Ph. 82nd Airborne.)

A Horsa glider has landed in a hedge in the Dutch countryside. (Ph. 82nd Airborne.)

General Gavin inspects his positions. (Ph. NA/D. François.)

Paratroopers from the 82nd pose next to a house in the Grave sector. (Ph. 82nd Airborne.)

A group of paratroopers from the *505th PIR.* (Ph. 82nd Airborne.)

One of the bridges before being taken during *Operation Market Garden,* this photograph shows the bridge over the river Maas at Grave. (Ph. 82nd Airborne.)

Below: Nijmegen bridge today. (Ph. 82nd Airborne.)

Two men from the 1st Battalion of the *505th* looking for German soldiers in the Goronne sector. (Ph. 82nd Airborne/D. François.)

Battle of the Ardennes

At Sissonne, the division received replacements to make up for the losses in the various regiments. The veterans of Normandy and Holland could finally have a short rest, even if training was soon to resume. Some paratroopers were even lucky enough to obtain a pass to go on leave to Reims, Paris or even England.

At the start of December, when most paratroopers from the 82nd thought they would soon be returning home, Christmas was looking bleak for the men of the « All American » ! Marshall Von Runstedt had decided otherwise!

Early in the morning of December 16, the Germans launched an unexpected offensive in the Belgian Ardennes. The American in the sector bravely defended their positions, but to no avail. The Germans broke through the lines, the Americans were caught completely by surprise.

With very few reserves available, Eisenhower decided to send his two airborne divisions, the 82nd and the 101st, to stabilize the rapidly deteriorating situation.

On December 17, Gavin's headquarters received orders from the Corps to urgently send the 82nd into the sector to contain the enemy counter-attack. The division had to be on the move within 24 hours. On December 18, one hour after morning dawned, the division was heading for Bastogne in Belgium. The « Screaming Eagles » of the 101st were to follow in the afternoon. The 82nd was attached to the 5th Corps and the 101st to the 8th Corps.

The 82nd grouped at Werbomont while the 101st set up camp at Bastogne.

From Werbomont, the division immediately started offensive operations to contain the German attacks.

Two paratroopers taking a short break in a forest in the Ardennes. (Ph. NA/D. François.)

On arrival, the men were faced with snow-covered forests and bitterly cold weather for this time of year.

The soldiers were not equipped to fight in these regions. Still wearing their jumpsuits, the paratroopers had no cold weather equipment. Armed only with individual weapons, they would have to repulse the German armored offensive.

In his memoirs, General Gavin described the situation he found on arriving at the front:

« I arrived at Werbomont at about 20h00 with the division's vehicles. A command post was quickly established on our arrival. Drivers and troops were exhausted, after two days without sleep.

The first enemy contact was made at Hablemont, where a road block had been set up by the 30th Division. A German armored reconnaissance party had broken through. I visited the locality and found five armored vehicles and some other vehicles. It appeared quite clear that the north-south road from Bastogne to Werbomont had been cut by the Germans in the vicinity of Houffalize.

The depth of this penetration was unknown, but there were rumors from truck drivers that the Germans were on the road, in the vicinity of Hotton. At 11h00, on December 19, orders were received to dispatch one infantry battalion and one platoon of Tank Destroyers to the area north of Hotton to block and clear all approaches from Hotton to the north, northwest and northeast.

During the afternoon of December 19, information and orders were received from Headquarters, 8th Corps (Airborne), which had been established about one mile north of Werbomont. The First Army was to hold along the general line Stoumont–Stavelot–Malmédy and counterattack in the direction of Trois-Ponts to halt the enemy's advance to the northwest.

In compliance with instructions received from corps headquarters, the 504th PIR advanced and seized the high ground northwest of Rahier, while the 505th PIR advanced and seized the high ground in the vicinity of Haut-Bodeux. The 508th PIR sent a company to the crossroads east of Bra. The rest of the regiment occupied the Chevron sector. The 325th GIR which had remained at Werbomont sent its third battalion to the vicinity of Barvaux and one company to the crossroads at Manhay.

These dispositions were consolidated during the night of December 19-20 and patrols pushed to the front to make contact with the enemy.

Shortly after daylight, 20 December, I met Colonel Reuben Tucker, 504th PIR commanding officer, in the town of Rahier. He had just received intelligence from civilians to the effect that approximately 125 vehicles, including 30 tanks, had moved through the town the afternoon before, heading towards Cheneux. I ordered Colonel Tucker to move into the town of Cheneux without delay and seize the bridge. It was imperative that the bridge should be seized intact.

Initial contact was made at the western exit of Cheneux by a patrol which had been sent from Rahier by the 1st battalion of the 504th. They fired on a German motorcyclist who was accompanied by a small patrol. This small patrol was followed by a company of Germans moving along the ridge, which turned out to be the advanced guard of the 1st SS Panzer Division. The 1st Battalion of the 504th drove them back outside Cheneux and set up camp in the town.

I went to the 505th PIR sector, where I found that the situation regarding the enemy was vague.

In the afternoon, I received orders from the 18th Corps to advance to the Vielsalm–Hebronval line …»

A German tank has been destroyed and its occupants taken prisoner. (Ph. NA/D. François.)

As General Gavin wrote in his memoirs, during the early hours of the Battle of the Ardennes, the situation was confused and enemy penetration unknown.

Over the next few days, the role of the 82nd was to contain this advance, then progressively reduce it.

At Saint Vith, the 82nd started to gain ground, with the 504th and the 325th taking the advantage in the attacks. The 504th PIR earned their second Presidential Unit Citation for their fighting at St.Vith, but at the cost of many lives.

The 101st was ordered to hold Bastogne, although they were surrounded. An air bridge was set up, enabling the besieged troops to hold their position. The « Screaming Eagle » paratroopers would have to spend Christmas in the shelters around the old town.

German prisoners are escorted by paratroopers from the 82nd. (Ph. NA/D. François.)

A paratrooper from the *505th PIR* eating a C ration. (Ph. NA/D. François.)

It was during the final phase of the Battle of the Ardennes, on January 29, that sergeant Leonard Funk of Co «C», *508th PIR*, was to earn his Congressional Medal of Honor. Funk led a platoon of men in the assault on Holzheim, and captured 80 German soldiers. Funk decided to leave his prisoners guarded by four of his paratroopers while the rest of his men continued to advance and eliminate the resistance in the village. In the meantime, three armed German soldiers arrived in the sector with American prisoners and found the group of German prisoners with their American guards. The three Germans, wearing white camouflage capes similar to those worn by the GIs, managed to disarm the four US guards. Funk and a few men returned to his group of prisoners. They quickly understood that there was something wrong. Taking advantage of their hesitation, the German officer went up to Funk and covered him with his MP 40. The German officer ordered the Americans to surrender. Funk, who still had his Tommy gun, and now with the German's MP 40 pressed against his stomach, tried to negotiate. Suddenly, he thrust the barrel of the machine pistol away from his stomach and, whipping his Tommy gun off his shoulder, shot the German dead. Funk overturned the situation, enabling his men to start fighting with the two Germans still armed and kill them. For this exploit, several months later Funk was awarded the highest decoration of the American Army for heroism by President Harry S. Truman at the White House.

The 4th Armored Division managed to enter Bastogne during the first week of January and relieve the 101st. The bulge was closed.

With the defeat of the counter-offensive in the Ardennes, the Third Reich lost over 220,000 men (110,000 were taken prisoner) and 1400 tanks. Last line of defense before Germany, the Rhine was to be more difficult to approach than to cross, under the harsh winter conditions.

Gavin's 82nd Division would have to launch the assault and enter the heart of Germany.

A paratrooper using his heavy helmet for a foot bath. (Ph. NA/D. François.)

Paratroopers from the *508th* have set up a .30-caliber machine gun on the edge of a field. (Ph. NA/D. François.)

A 75 mm gun. (Ph. NA/D. François.)

These paratroopers seem to be praying in front of a crucifix in the Ardennes. (Ph. NA/D. François.)

In spite of the cold, a few paratroopers from the 82nd have organized a musical show for their comrades. (Ph. NA/D. François.)

MPs of the 82nd guarding prisoners. (Ph. NA/D. François.)

Paratroopers from the 80th AA have set up a 57 mm gun. (Ph. NA/D. François.)

2 Recon boys in the Bulge Dec 1944 (handwritten)

1

2

1. Armored jeep from the reconnaissance unit of the 82nd. (Ph. NA/D. François.)

2. A jeep from the *Signal Company*. (Ph. NA/D. François.)

3. A German tank on fire, hit by an antitank shell. (Ph. NA/D. François.)

4. Two dead soldiers from the *Waffen-SS*. (Ph. NA/D. François.)

3

4

Three young soldiers from the *Waffen-SS*, now POWs. (Ph. NA/D. François.)

Paratroopers have captured German soldiers and will use them as a human shield to cross open ground. (Ph. NA/D. François.)

Two German soldiers have been killed in the explosion of an American shell. (Ph. NA/D. François.)

A few souvenirs of Captain William Nation from the *508th PIR*, killed on January 30, 1945, in Belgium. (Ph. D. François.)

Winter 1945 in the Ardennes was one of the harshest winters. (Ph. NA/D. François.)

Captain William Nation, from the 508th Airborne Regiment. (Ph. D. François.)

A German soldier, freezing cold through lack of winter equipment, has been taken prisoner. (Ph. NA/D. François.)

Above: firing point for men of the 508th. (Ph. NA/D. François.)

Opposite: soldiers from the 325th advancing through the snow-covered forests of the Belgian Ardennes. (Ph. NA/D. François.)

Above: General Montgomery and General Ridgway. (Ph. NA/D. François.)

Opposite: a Tiger tank has been destroyed by an antitank gun. (Ph. NA/D. François.)

MPs inspect the vehicles, enemy paratroopers wearing American uniforms have been reported. (Ph. NA/D. François.)

Religious ceremony of the 3rd Battalion from the *508th PIR*. (Ph. NA/D. François.)

The *254th Field Artillery* opens fire with a 155 mm gun. (Ph. NA/D. François.)

A few men from the 325th after an attack. (Ph. NA/D. François.)

Men from the *325th GIR* are issued greatcoats to protect them against the cold. (Ph. NA/D. François.)

The 325th advancing through the mist and cold of the Ardennes. (Ph. NA/D. François.)

1. Men from the 504th walking along a road. Opposite, a 57 mm anti-tank gun. (Ph. NA/D. François.)

2. The 505th has taken numerous prisoners. (Ph. NA/D. François.)

Above: paratroopers from the 517th Airborne Regiment (17th Airborne) are suffering the same difficulties as their comrades from the 82nd. This photographs shows the Saint Vith road. (Ph. NA/D. François.)

Opposite: the *Service Company of the 505th*. (Ph. NA/D. François.)

Opposite: an M36 tank from the *703rd Tank Destroyer Battalion* has been destroyed by an enemy tank. (Ph. NA/D. François.)

Below: a Sherman tank from the *740th Bn* advancing with men from the 82nd. (Ph. NA/D. François.)

Above: an M36 tank from the *703rd TD* Bn has taken up position in a village. (Ph. NA/D. François.)

Below: a tank from the *740th Bn* attached to the 82nd. (Ph. NA/D. François.)

Tanks from the *740th Bn* attached to the 82nd, in the center an armored reconnaissance jeep. (Ph. NA/D. François.)

A tank from the *740th Bn* seems to have been damaged. (Ph. NA/D. François.)

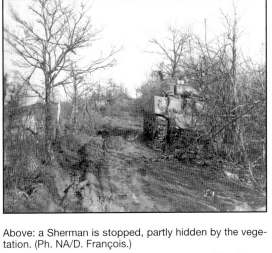

Above: a Sherman is stopped, partly hidden by the vegetation. (Ph. NA/D. François.)

Below: men from the 740th have set up a provisional command post in a public building. (Ph. NA/D. François.)

An antitank shell has destroyed the track of this tank from the *740th Battalion*. (Ph. NA/D. François.)

1. Men from Battery B of the 376th load a 75 mm gun. (Ph. NA/D. François.)

2. Paratroopers from the 82nd receive news from home, thanks to the Army newspaper, the Stars & Stripes. (Ph. NA/D. François.)

3. A German soldier lying near a jeep. Due to the fierce fighting and the cold, it was impossible to bury the dead quickly. (Ph. D. François.)

4. Colonel Ekman, commanding the *505th PIR*. (Ph. 82nd Airborne.)

5. Donuts in ammunition boxes are distributed to men from the 82nd. (Ph. NA/D. François.)

6. Paratroopers have set up position on a hillside. (Ph. NA/D. François.)

7. General Gavin meets officers from his staff. (Ph. 82nd Airborne.)

8. The General visits the men from the 3rd Battalion of the *505th PIR*. (Ph. NA/D. François.)

9. Like his men, Gavin lives in the field. (Ph. 82nd Airborne.)

10. Gavin always carries his Garand. (Ph. NA/D. François.)

1. German prisoner at Fosse on January 4, 1945. (Ph. NA/D. François.)

2. Like the GIs of the 82nd, the German soldiers are poorly equipped to face the severe weather conditions. (Ph. NA/D. François.)

3. German soldiers have just been taken prisoner, one of them is still carrying his weapon. (Ph. NA/D. François.)

4. A paratrooper praying, during a break. (Ph. NA/D. François.)

5. Back in France at the Sissonne camp, a paratrooper from the *508th PIR* poses, like many of his comrades, beside the "wishing well". (Ph. D. François.)

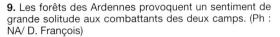

6. Chargement d'un canon de 75 mm. (Ph : NA/ D. François)

7. Lt.-Colonel John Norton. (Ph : 82nd Airborne)

8. *Pvt.* Lesage, *Medic* au *508th PIR* devant le « puits des songes » à Sissone. (Ph : D. François)

9. Les forêts des Ardennes provoquent un sentiment de grande solitude aux combattants des deux camps. (Ph : NA/ D. François)

10. Des officiers de la 82e reçoivent des mains du général Brereton la DSC. (Ph : 82nd Airborne)

11. Des hommes de la 82e progressent sur une route enneigée de Belgique. (Ph : 82nd Airborne)

12. Un para escorte vers l'arrière des prisonniers allemands. (Ph : D. François)

Men from the 307th Air-borne Engineer Battalion push a German tank off the road. (Ph. NA/D. François.)

1. *Pvt.* Henri Gavazza from the *508th PIR* in front of the «wishing well» at Sissone. (Ph. D. François.)

2. *Pvt.* Ralph Perico from the 508th, who has just spend a harsh winter in the Ardennes, taking a well-earned rest at Sissonne. (Ph. D. François.)

3. A paratrooper from the 505th armed with a Thompson subma-chine gun. (Ph. NA/D. François.)

A Panther tank has been knocked out by a P-47 aircraft in the Cheneux sector. (Ph. NA/D. François.)

Men from the 325th advancing deep in the Ardennes. (Ph. NA/D. François.)

Pvt. R.J Whiteman in front of a destroyed Panther. (Ph. 82nd Airborne.)

Religious service. (Ph. 82nd Airborne.)

Lieutenant Colonel Smith from the *507th PIR* in front of his battalion. (Ph. D. François.)

Two radio operators from the 82nd have set up their transmitter in a barn in the Werbomont sector. (Ph. NA/D. François.)

German prisoners of war are held temporarily in a ruined garage by two MPs from the 82nd, before being evacuated to the rear. (Ph. NA/D. François.)

Back in France after the Battle of the Ardennes, the *507th PIR,* which had been attached to the *17th Airborne Division*, is received by the mayor of a small village. (Ph. D. François.)

Germany

Back in France, the *82nd Airborne Division* returned to the Sissonne camp. In April 1945, it left the camp for Cologne, to take part in an operation along the Rhine code-named the « Ruhr pocket » where 350.000 German soldiers under the command of Marshall Model were surrounded.

This was a new mission for the *82nd Airborne Division* since the objective was to take a static defensive position, taking a line on the west bank of the Rhine including the town of Cologne. Apart from a few artillery or mortar barrages and patrols sent across the Rhine, the division's mission was relatively peaceful. The paratroopers spent their time forming music groups with instruments « found » in the town, repairing a few bicycles and motorcycles; huge stocks of wine and beer were discovered.

On April 6, Co « A » of the *504th PIR* and a section from Co « C » of the *307th AEB* received orders to cross the Rhine on boats and land at Hitdorf. They had hardly disembarked from the boats when Tucker's men made contact with the enemy, as they landed in a mine field. Firmly entrenched in bunkers, the enemy opened fire. The paratroopers were lucky enough to knock out several machine guns. After setting up a defensive position, they managed to enter Hitdorf. By 08h30, the village had been cleared of all enemy forces and 68 prisoners were lined up on the village beach.

The Germans then launched several counter-attacks to recapture the village; they were to be pushed back. After several attempts, the Germans supported by tanks and covered by a smoke screen managed to encircle several American positions. Under a deluge of artillery fire, the men from Co « A » had to pull back along the Rhine. Here, the two sections of Co « A » established a horseshoe defense position. At 1h30 the next morning, two sections of Co « I » arrived to reinforce their comrades and repulsed a new German attack composed of over 200 infantry and a platoon of tanks. The two companies withdrew to the other side of the Rhine, taking with them thirteen more prisoners. A total of 80 Germans were taken prisoner and 350 were either killed or wounded.

Shortly after taking Hitdorf, the German resistance in the Ruhr pocket collapsed and the division was able to enjoy a moment's respite.

But once again, however, the division was requested to support the Second British Army, along the river Elbe in the province of Mecklenburg. On April 30, 1945, the *82nd Airborne Division* crossed the Elbe at Bleckede. This was to be the division's 11th and bridgehead, and the last.

The men from the reconnaissance section of the *505th PIR* led the assault. The « All American » advanced more than 6 miles (10 kilometers) behind enemy lines. Later, the *504th* and the *325th* crossed the positions held by the *505th* and the next evening, they were able to push forward more than 32 miles (52 km), helped by the *7th Armored Division* (British) and the *740th Tank Battalion*. The division took several tens of thousands of prisoners and waited for contact with the Russians. On May 3, 1945, the *82nd Airborne Division* made contact with the Russians, putting an end to the war. The war was officially ended five days later, on May 8, 1945.

Paratroopers from the *82nd Airborne Division* had taken part in jumps during operations: in Sicily, Italy, Normandy and Holland, and a boat landing at Anzio, a total of 371 days fighting in six different countries. It was at this time that the division was chosen to represent the United States in the Berlin sector. The 508th, which had served with the division since Normandy, was selected by Eisenhower to become his Guard of Honor at Frankfurt am Main. The « Red Devils » of the *508th* remained as occupation force after the 82nd had gone back to the United States and were to return home in November 1946.

Between May and July 1945, all the veterans who had obtained sufficient points were transferred to the *17th Airborne Division* before being demobilized. The army had developed a system of points based on the number of days fighting, decorations, citations and injuries. Soldiers with more than 100 points could ask to be sent home.

After the end of the war, the 82nd was transferred to Epinal in eastern France, where replacements took the place of the demobilized soldiers. Many of these replacements had served with the 101st and the 17th and still wore their division's shoulder patch.

In July, the division was transferred to Berlin as occupation force for a period of five months. During this time, numerous officials from all the allied nations visited the division, especially during a demonstration jump on Tempelhof airport. The 82nd did not just attract political and military personalities, however. Numerous stars also wanted to meet these new soldiers: Bob Hope, Ingrid Bergman, Frank Sinatra and of course Marlene Dietrich were welcomed at the headquarters of the «*All American*» division.

On January 3, 1946, back in the United States, General James Gavin marched at the head of his division up 5th Avenue in New York during the Victory Parade, where the soldiers from the 82nd Airborne were given a welcome fit for heroes.

Three paratroopers from the *508th PIR* pose in front of the « wishing well » at Sissonne. Sgt. Bob Speers is at the center. (Ph. D. François.)

1. *Pvt.* Lou Horn, after serving with the *507th PIR*. He was to be transferred to the *505th PIR* which he joined in Germany. Here, in front of the headquarters at Berlin. (Ph. D. François.)

2. Like their comrades from the 82nd, these paratroopers from the 507th now attached to the *17th Airborne Division* are assigned as occupation force in Germany. (Ph. D. François.)

3. Company K of the *325th GIR* at Epinal in France. (Ph. D. François.)

Co. K 325 GLIDER INFANTRY
82ND AIRBORNE DIV.

EPINAL
FRA

3

Generals Eisenhower, Ridgway and Brereton during a parade in Germany. (Ph. D. François.)

General Brereton, commanding the 1st Allied Airborne Army with General Ridgway, commanding the 8th Airborne Corps. (Ph. D. François.)

Victory Parade of the *82nd Airborne Division*. (Ph. D. François.)

Airborne troops on parade in Germany. (Ph. D. François.)

Ike and Gavin at Frankfurt. (Ph. D. François.)

508th on parade at Frankfurt. The regiment was selected to be General Eisenhower's Guard of Honor. (Ph. D. François.)

Marlene Dietrich, she was to become the « godmother » of the *82nd Airborne Division* and had a liaison with General Gavin. (Ph. D. François.)

Inspection of the *508th PIR* at Frankfurt. (Ph. D. François.)

General Gavin awarding the DSC to *Sgt*. Funk, who was to receive the Congressional Medal of Honor a few months later. Leonard Funk was the most highly decorated soldier of the *82d Airborne Division*. (Ph. D. François.)

Monty visits the *82d Airborne Division*, during a short stay in Germany. (Ph. D. François.)

1. Headquarters of the 3rd Battalion, *508th PIR* in Germany with the division's emblem. (Ph. D. François.)

2. Lieutenant Colonel Louis Mendez fastening the fourragere to the flag of the *508th PIR*. (Ph. D. François.)

3. A company of the 3rd Battalion, *508th PIR* at Frankfurt. (Ph. D. François.)

1. Another view of the headquarters of the 3rd Battalion, *508th PIR*. (Ph. D. François.)

5. CP of Co « G » from the 3rd Battalion, 508th *PIR* in Germany. (Ph. D. François.)

6. This photograph shows the paratroopers from the *508th PIR* who, during the course of the war, were taken prisoner and managed to escape. Jack Schlegel is the second in the first row. (Ph. D. François.)

1. A paratrooper from the 82nd posing at the door of an aircraft for a photographer. (Ph. D. François.)

2. A group of paratroopers from the *508th PIR* waiting to board for a practice jump in Germany. (Ph. D. François.)

3. A paratrooper from the 508th during a transfer in a C-47. (Ph. D. François.)

274

Sgt. Bob Speers (on the right) with his men. (Ph. D. François.)

Regimental football team. (Ph. D. François.)

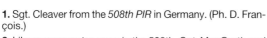

1. Sgt. Cleaver from the *508th PIR* in Germany. (Ph. D. François.)

2. Like many paratroopers in the 508th, *Sgt.* MacGrath and his comrade adopted the red beret of the English paratroopers. (Ph. D. François.)

3. *Sgt.* MacGrath sitting in front of Co « G » sign. (Ph. D. François.)

4. MacGrath swapped his cap for a British paratrooper's beret. (Ph. D. François.)

Sgt. George MacGrath ready for a practice jump in Germany. (Ph. D. François.)

Cleaver with two comrades from the 508th. (Ph. D. François.)

Sgt. George MacGrath from the *508th PIR*, who took part in the regiment's three campaigns. (Ph. D. François.)

The Post-War Period

Back in the United States, the *82nd Airborne Division* was invited to take part in big parades throughout the country, like this one in Washington. (Ph. D. François.)

After the chaos of the Second World War, two major powers seemed to emerge from the other allied countries. America and the USSR, separated by diametrically opposed ideologies, prepared to face each other in a war that appeared to be inevitable.

Back home, the *82d Airborne Division* started a series of training exercises designed to resist a landing force or to fight under conditions of extreme cold. The Soviet bloc had become the new enemy.

In June 1950, North Korea decided to cross the 38th parallel and invade South Korea. General Douglas MacArthur, Commander of United States Army Forces, suggested first sending the *82d Airborne Division* to Korea, since it was the only combat-ready division, currently in « strategic reserve ».

This was not to be the case and finally the *187th ARTC* of the *11th Airborne Division* was sent to Inchon in September 1950. A few months later, it was to make two jumps in operation.

In 1958, the *8th Corps*, to which the 82nd was attached, was assigned as strategic army corps and therefore as rapid deployment force. With this new doctrine, the training of the « All American » division was adapted to suit the requirements of its new mission. During the Cuban missile crisis in 1962, the need for a force of this type became apparent. The presence of Soviet missiles with nuclear warheads on Cuba, less than 100 miles (150 kilometers) from the American coast was unacceptable for the Kennedy government, which prepared for war.

President John F. Kennedy was determined to remove this threat to his country's security. Nuclear war between the two super-powers became a real possibility. A diplomatic marathon followed, where exchange proposals alternated with threats. Finally, Kennedy sent an ultimatum to Moscow: either withdraw the missiles or American forces would invade Cuba. This project would involve the airborne assault of the 8th Corps with the 82nd and 101st Airborne Divisions. Fortunately, the Russians decided to back down, after a semblance of negotiation to avoid losing face.

In the spring of 1965, the Dominican Republic in the Caribbean was torn apart by civil war, inspired by Cuban communism. Over one thousand civilians were killed during the first few weeks of rioting.

American citizens and US interests were under considerable threat, President Lyndon Johnson had no alternative but to send the *82nd Airborne Division* to protect these citizens and American property on the island.

The 82nd was sent into combat for the first time since 1945. Code named « Power Pack », the division prepared to deploy its forces nearly 1000 miles (1500 kilometers) away from its bases. Finally, the 1st Battalion of the 508th was selected to land first on San Isidro airfield at 01h30 during the night of **April 29, 1965**. During the next few hours, 33 C-130 troop transport planes brought the rest of the 3rd Brigade and its support units.

Shortly after landing and taking control of the airfield, the 1st Battalion assisted by the 1st Battalion of the 17th *Calvary* Regiment and the 307th Airborne Engineer Battalion deployed rapidly to secure Duarte Bridge, a strategic point for the operation. This bridge was the only link between the airfield and the capital Santo Domingo. It had to be held at any cost. This marked the first contact with the rebels, and the most violent fighting. The bridge was taken the next day. The following day the paratroopers had to make contact the embassy. The mission was accomplished with the loss of only one paratrooper, the Division's first victim since WW2. The rest of the Division landed during May, remaining until the Brazilian forces from the United Nations arrived. Unfortunately, just as the situation appeared to be stabilizing, the pro-Castro rebels launched an offensive and managed to reach the defenses of the 82nd. The division lost a total of about 60 men.

Viet-Nam

5

Since the start of the Cold War with the Soviet Union, American policy has been to contain the expansion of Communism throughout the world whenever possible, and more especially in the less developed nations. The former French colony of South-East Asia, Indochina, has just become independent after a long and bloody war, ending with the defeat of the Dien Bien Phu entrenched camp.

Following the Geneva Accords of the 17th parallel, the country is now split into two: the Republic of South Vietnam, whose capital is Saigon, and Communist North Vietnam, whose capital is Hanoi. A guerilla war developed in the south between the communist rebels, the Viet Cong (known as the Viet Minh under French occupation) and the Army of the Republic of Vietnam (ARVN). The Viet-Congs wanted to convert the rural population in the south to communism and destabilize the President Diem's authority.

US involvement in South Vietnam started in 1961 under the Kennedy administration, when several hundred military advisers from the Special Forces were flown in. By the end of 1965, 185,000 American soldiers were in Vietnam, two years later the number had increased to 465,000.

The communists decided to launch a series of major offensives across South Vietnam during the 1968 celebrations of the "Têt Nguyên Dan" (Lunar New Year Day), which came to be known as the Tet Offensive. Taken by surprise by this sudden and unexpected attack, the ARVN called on the allied forces for immediate support. General William Westmoreland, Commander of Military Assistance Command in Vietnam, decided to ask the United States for reinforcements, more especially from the 82nd Airborne Division.

The division's 3rd Brigade, comprised of the 1st and 2nd Battalions of the 505th PIR, the 1st Battalion of the 508th PIR, the division artillery and its support units formed the division's rapid action force. On February 12, 1968, the 3rd Bridge was alerted for deployment. The first echelon took off from Pope Air Force Base on board C-141 aircraft, heading first for Japan before reaching its destination in Chu Lai, Vietnam, under the command of Colonel Alexander Bolling.

The rest of the brigade arrived in Vietnam between 14 and 24 February.

At the end of the month, General Westmoreland called a meeting with Colonel Bolling to discuss the urgent need to transfer the division to the Hue sector, where the enemy had gained ground. On March 1, the division set out in convoy toward this sector along the infamous Highway 1. On several occa-

Fat City Camp, Sgt. Leoncio Quiles from the 505th PIR is firing with an M-60 machine gun mounted on a jeep. This camp is 5 miles (8 km) from Chu Lai. (Ph. NA/D. François.)

Sunset over the entrenched camp. (Ph. NA/D. François.)

sions, the convoy came under fire from mortars and small arms. On site, the "All American" set up a base camp which it called Camp Rodriguez, in tribute to staff-sergeant Joe Rodriguez, killed by a booby trap during a patrol at Chu Lai.

The brigade's mission was straightforward: stop any attempts by the enemy to recapture the former capital, Hue. Secret service reports had predicted an imminent attack in the sector.

On March 9, the brigade was placed under the orders of the 101st Airborne Division and Operation Carentan I started. The operation was designed to wipe out the 4th North-Vietnamese Regiment hiding in the paddy fields south of Hue. It was during this mission that the 1st Battalion of the 505th PIR received its baptism of fire. Within a few days, the enemy had fallen back and taken refuge in the jungle.

The brigade was reorganized and detached from the 101st Airborne Division, becoming an independent light infantry brigade.

The brigade then took part in Operation Nevada Eagle which started on May 17 and lasted throughout the summer of 68. The Battle of Route 547 followed operation Nevada Eagle. The enemy seemed to be pulling back to its base camps in the jungle to regroup and pick up provisions. With Hue back under control, the brigade and units from the 101st could start operations deep in the jungle and destroy the Viet Cong on their bases.

On May 21, Camp Rodriguez was attacked during the night. A Viet Cong group had managed to set up mortars and launched an attack with a hundred men in a suicide mission. The attack was held off and many Vietnamese soldiers killed. Fortunately, none of the paratroopers of the 82nd was injured.

In October 1968, the 3rd Brigade was redeployed on the 3rd Corps Tactical Zone and assigned responsibility for the region west of the South Vietnamese capital, Saigon. In this new sector, its mission was to prevent any infiltration by the VC and stop any attack on Saigon town center.

Using a new tactic which consisted in fighting when the enemy is active, the paratroopers from the 82nd decided to rest during the day and infiltrate and fight during the night. The result was immediate. Viet Cong and North Vietnamese leaders were killed in ambushes and others captured during their nighttime movements. On December 17, 1968, General Bolling placed the brigade under the command of General George W. Dickerson, in a ceremony at Camp Red Ball.

The brigade was now covering a wider sector, along the Cambodian border and on the Delta, as a Battalion Combat Team.

In September 1969, the 82nd conducted its last combat operation in Vietnam - Yorktown Victor - with the 1st Infantry Division and South Vietnamese troops. The mission consisted in destroying an important enemy complex in the north of Saigon, known as the "Iron Triangle". This sector was riddled with tunnels, underground bunkers and buried supply caches. The 3rd Brigade paratroopers captured huge quantities of weapons and munitions. Numerous enemy soldiers were killed, either taken by surprise or while trying to retaliate. Most American casualties were caused by booby traps set up in the tunnels.

In October 1969, the brigade started its return to Fort Bragg, having serving 22 months in Vietnam. 212 paratroopers of the "All American" were killed in action.

On December 12, 1969 the entire division paid tribute to its dead, in a moving ceremony held at Fort Bragg.

Whatever the place, whatever the mission, the paratroopers of the 82nd Airborne demonstrated, once
again, their professionalism.

Like all operations in Vietnam, the helicopter is omnipre-
sent and has replaced jumps in action. (Ph. NA/D. François.)

An NCO of the 82nd, Master Sergeant Charles Wunderlick, takes the long journey between Fort Bragg and Vietnam, February 16, 1968. (Ph. NA/D. François.)

Arrival of the 3rd Brigade at Chu Lai airport. (Ph. NA/D. François.)

Paratroopers from the 3rd Brigade of the 82nd land in Vietnam in February 1968. (Ph. NA/D. François.)

1. Colonel Alexander Bolling arrives at Chu Lai with his 3rd Brigade on February 19, 1968. (Ph. NA/D. François.)

2. The first elements of the 82nd Airborne Division arrive in Vietnam on February 14, 1968. (Ph. D. François.)

3. Men and equipment from the 1st Battalion of the 508th PIR leaving a C-141 at Chu Lai. (Ph. NA/D. François.)

1. Paratroopers from the 3rd Brigade of the 82nd land in Vietnam. They were to stay twelve months. (Ph. NA/D. François.)

2. The 3rd Brigade arrives at Chu Lai, the men are lined up near the aircraft. (NA/DF.)

3. Chu Lai, arrival of the 3rd Brigade of the 82nd Airborne Division. This photograph shows members of Co "C" of the 1st Battalion, 505th PIR. (Ph. NA/D. François.)

4. Chu Lai, departure of the 3rd Brigade. (Ph. NA/D. François.)

Men and equipment from the 1st Battalion of the 508th PIR landing at Chu Lai. (NA/DF.)

Arrival of the 3rd Brigade at Chu Lai. The vehicles are line up ready to go. (Ph. NA/D. François.)

Paratroopers from the 82nd Airborne Division leaving the airport en route for Camp Rodriguez. (Ph. NA/D. François.)

On arrival, men from the "All American" receive training on the booby traps they are likely to encounter in Vietnam. (Ph. NA/D. François.)

An instructor from the Special Forces showing them a booby trap. (Ph. NA/D. François.)

Battery "A" of the 2nd Bn., 321st Field Artillery Regiment, firing with a 105 mm Howitzer, February 22, 1968. (Ph. NA/D. François.)

A paratrooper from the 505th PIR helping install the defenses of a bunker to secure the Fat City base camp, 5 miles (8 km) from Chu Lai. (Ph. NA/D. François.)

Sgt. Willie Jones from the 505th PIR surveys the sector while his comrades are resting. (Ph. NA/D. François.)

1. Phu Bai base camp, General Alexander Bolling is talking with General Barsanti from the 101st Airborne Division. (Ph. NA/D. François.)

2. Phu Bai camp, SP Sergeant Edward Ridwood guards the camp entrance. (Ph. NA/D. François.)

3. Construction of a casemate at Phu Bai, March 6, 1968. (Ph. NA/D. François.)

Men from the 3rd Brigade filling sandbags to reinforce their position. (Ph. NA/D. François.)

4. Phu Bai camp, Pfc Walther Liebelt surveys the perimeter around the 3rd Brigade command post. (Ph. NA/D. François.)

5. Phu Bai camp, Sgt. Roger Avery calculates the firing direction for his M-60 machine gunners. (Ph. NA/D. François.)

6. Phu Bai base camp, paratroopers from the 3rd Brigade filling sandbags to protect a bunker. (Ph. NA/D. François.)

7. Sunset over Phu Bai base camp. (Ph. NA/D. François.)

8. Phu Bai, Lt. Col. Alfred Zamperlli congratulates the men from the 3rd Brigade for their achievements during their stay in Vietnam, October 28, 1969. (Ph. NA/D. François.)

Men from Co "B" of the 1st Battalion 505th PIR advancing over uncovered terrain during a "Search and Destroy" mission, March 25, 1968. (Ph. NA/D. François.)

"Search and Destroy" mission, infiltration in enemy territory is carried out using helicopters. (Ph. NA/D. François.)

1. Choppers landing men during the "Search and Destroy" mission. (NA/DF.)

2. Private Willie Grayson from the 1st Battalion 505th PIR watching the rear while his comrades search a straw hut, March 28, 1968. (Ph. NA/D. François.)

3. "Search and Destroy" mission 300 miles (500 km) from Saigon. (Ph. NA/D. François.)

4. Elements from the 3rd Brigade carrying out a "Search and Destroy" operation supported by armored personnel carriers in the village of Thon Vuoug Phan, Thu Thien Province, 5 miles (8 km) south of Hue. (Ph. NA/D. François.)

A paratrooper firing an M-60 machine gun on a Viet Cong position. (Ph. NA/D. François.)

A patrol launching an assault on the last Viet Cong positions during operation "Hawthorne". (Ph. NA/D. François.)

A paratrooper wearing 'tiger stripes' camouflage gear and armed with an M-16 inspects a tunnel entrance. (Ph. NA/D. François.)

Paratroopers from the 82nd preparing their equipment ready for an operation. The red patch on the helmet is the identification sign of paratroopers from the 82nd. (Ph. NA/D. François.)

Operation "MacArthur", a sergeant from the reconnaissance unit of the 173rd Airborne Brigade checks the positions of friendly troops on Hill 800. (Ph. NA/D. François.)

293

An officer sending the coordinates of enemy positions by radio, to obtain artillery support. (Ph. D. François.)

This soldier is carrying a radio set and two smoke grenades. (Ph. NA/D. François.)

Base camp of the 82nd and command center. A corporal requesting artillery support by radio. (Ph. NA/D. François.)

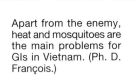

Apart from the enemy, heat and mosquitoes are the main problems for GIs in Vietnam. (Ph. D. François.)

The GIs quickly learn jungle survival techniques. (Ph. NA/D. François.)

Nha Trang, an NCO in the Special Forces, instructing paratroopers from a C-130 fuselage. (Ph. NA/D. François.)

Above: Dong Ba Thin, a instructor from the 5th Special Forces, checks the equipment of a paratrooper at jump school. (Ph. NA/D. François.)

Opposite: practice jump at Nha Trang. (Ph. NA/D. François.)

A Special Forces instructor checks the equipment of a paratrooper. (Ph. NA/D. François.)

Dong Ba Thin, a Special Forces sergeant gives instructions to the paratroopers about to make a practice jump. (Ph. NA/D. François.)

1. A UH-1D helicopter about to land on an LZ. (Ph. NA/D. François.)

2. Paratroopers leaving a UH-1D helicopter. (Ph. NA/D. François.)

3. Troop transport for an operation. (Ph. NA/D. François.)

4. Medivac (medical evacuation) of a paratrooper injured in action. (Ph. NA/D. François.)

Operation with helicopter support. (Ph. NA/D. François.)

Helicopters have replaced jumps in operation. (Ph. NA/D. François.)

1. Reconnaissance mission for a team from the 5th SF, led by Lt. Jay. D. Richard. (Ph. NA/D. François.)

2. Patrol along a paddy field on the edge of a village. (Ph. NA/D. François.)

3. Elements from the 82nd walking through a paddy field. (Ph. NA/D. François.)

A member of the reconnaissance section of the 1st Bat., 327th Regiment, equipped with an AN/PRC-25 crossing a paddy field. (Ph. NA/D. François.)

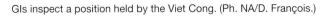

GIs inspect a position held by the Viet Cong. (Ph. NA/D. François.)

Track built by the Viet Cong along a hillside. (Ph. NA/D. François.)

Sgt Curtis Pitts from Co "B" of the 505th PIR participating in a raid on a village destroyed some time before, March 25, 1968. (Ph. NA/D. François.)

Viet Congs were hiding in the village. (Ph. NA/D. François.)

The village is searched, there could be a cache of weapons hidden in a straw hut. (Ph. NA/D. François.)

A cache of weapons has just been discovered behind the village. (Ph. NA/D. François.)

302

Weapons were hidden in the village, it is destroyed. (Ph. NA/D. François.)

Villages hiding Viet Congs are systematically burnt down. (Ph. D. François.)

Peasants are searched and interrogated. (Ph. NA/D. François.)

Paratroopers have taken a prisoner, he will be handed over to the ARVN. (Ph. NA/D. François.)

An MP from the 82nd picking up a prisoner's documents. (Ph. D. François.)

Viet prisoners will be taken to the camp for interrogation before being transferred to a prisoners' camp. (Ph. NA/D. François.)

Paratroopers waiting for confirmation of the identities of villager-partisans on the registers of Binh Dink Province. (Ph. NA/D. François.)

Pfc. Timothy Moses from the 508th PIR cleaning one of his company's .50-caliber machine guns. (Ph. NA/D. François.)

A paratrooper calculating a bearing. (Ph. NA/D. François.)

Sgt. Paul Narce, from Co "A" of the 505th PIR eating a ration beside a bunker. (Ph. NA/D. François.)

Lt. Freeman Johnson giving Sgt. Leonard Avery (505th PIR) his pay. (Ph. NA/D. François.)

A paratrooper from the 3rd Brigade readings news from home. (Ph. NA/D. François.)

Sunset over a strong-point, the GI is armed with an M-14. (Ph. NA/D. François.)

6

Grenada and Panama

After leading his country to independence from Britain in 1974 when it became a member of the Commonwealth, Sir Eric Gairy was appointed Prime Minister of Grenada. He was ousted five years later in a bloodless coup led by Maurice Bishop.

The new leader set up the Provisional Revolutionary Government (PRG) of Grenada, based on communist ideology.

Western states were alarmed by Bishop's policy, when he invited a large contingent of Cuban workers to build a new international airport at Point Salines. This project had a twofold objective: firstly, attract tourists to Grenada and, secondly, build an airfield for Cuban troops flying out to support the communist cause in Africa.

In October 1983, the People's Revolutionary Army (PRA) invaded Grenada: Maurice Bishop and four of his ministers were arrested and executed.

On 21 October, the leaders of six small nations forming the Organization of Eastern Caribbean States met at Bridgetown, Barbados, to consider joint military action against Grenada. The United States immediately answered the request for assistance, mainly concerned by the safety of 1000 American citizens, including 800 students. US naval vessels on maneuvers in the Mediterranean were diverted to Grenada. Special detachment 124, comprising the helicopter carrier USS Guam and four "landing" escorts of Amphibious squadron 4, carrying 1700 marines of the 22nd Marine Amphibious Unit (MAU) ready for action, with landing craft, tanks and amphibious tractors aboard, was diverted from its route and ordered to head for Grenada. USS Guam also carried aircraft from Marine Medium Helicopter Squadron 261 (Reinforced) (HMM- 261). The second task force consisted of a number of aircraft carriers led by the carrier USS Independence. No major airborne assault was planned, but two Ranger battalions could be dropped on the former airport at Pearl in the north east of the island which, hopefully by this time, should have been taken by the Marines. Small teams of Navy Seals and Army Delta Force paratroopers were also ordered to lead the jump in the major air-sea assault using HALO paratroopers (High Altitude, Low Opening), whose mission was to carry out raids and reconnaissance operations, including checking the state of the new runway under construction at Point Salines, nearly 10 000 feet (3 km) long. The 1st and 2nd Battalions of the 75th Ranger Regiment were placed on alert at Fort Lewis and Fort Stewart.

The rapid deployment force of the 82nd Airborne Division at Fort Bragg was ordered to prepare for transport to Grenada. The mission, after capturing Pearl, was to secure the capital, St George, free the Governor General, locate and evacuate American citizens and clean up any members of the People's Revolutionary Army on the 133-sq mile (344 sq km) island. This last mission included fighting against Cubans, who had joined the PRA, and securing the new Point Saline runway which was long enough for the Lockheed C-141A Starlifters coming to evacuate the American civilians.

During the predawn hours of 24 October the Navy Seals landed on the beach, the first Americans to set foot in Grenada. Seal and Delta Force paratroopers jumped the same night, but four Seals, ordered to land at Point Salines, were dropped in the sea. Caught up in their parachutes, the four men drowned. On October 25 at 05h00, the Marines landed in amphibious vehicles to prepare for the attack on Pearl airport, with the initial objective of securing the northern section of the island. They were faced with no resistance. The airfield was captured by the Marines at about 07h25, just in time to welcome the Rangers jumping from Lockheed C130s.

The drop zone at Pearl airport a long narrow strip, flanked on one side by he sea. Due to the strong wind blowing over the island the Rangers, loaded with as much ammunition as they could carry in their backpacks, would have to make a low altitude jump. The weapons and ammunition were fastened to the parachute harness with snap-links. The new MC-1 parachutes had been swapped for the old T-10s, considered as safer at low altitude. At the last minute, the Rangers were ordered to remove their reserve chutes, since they would be jumping with a heavier load than usual. About to jump from the leading aircraft, Lieutenant-Colonel Ralph Hagler, commander of the 2nd Battalion of Rangers, looked back quickly towards his men and told them to be brave, before jumping from an altitude of 470 feet (143 m) in a 25 mph wind (40 km/h).

The men first met with stiff resistance from the ground forces, until two companies of Marines were loaded into 13 amphibious assault vehicles landed at Grand Mal, behind the enemy forced. The two Ranger battalions then headed towards the Cuban camp, where they easily captured the defenders. The combined force of Marines and Rangers headed southwards to meet up north of St George, before the Marines captured the Governor General's residence and the Rangers the radio station.

The PRA fighters now concentrated their forces in the island on Forts Rupert, Matthew and Frederick. The last sector was the nerve center of the PRA, and all efforts to capture them were stymied. On the second day of the invasion, the Marines and Rangers conducted a combined helicopter assault on the campus south of St George, and found most of the American students. Navy Boeing Vertol CH-46 Sea Knights were used to evacuate the students from the college complex. In the meantime, a company of Marines successfully attacked the Fort Frederick command center.

Resistance from the revolutionary forces was now only sporadic and disorganized.

The 2nd brigade of the 82nd Airborne Division led by Major General Edward L. Trobaugh, which had touched down at Point Salines at 14h00 on D day, was now in the process of cleaning up the island. When the three units of the American land force met at St George, on the third day of operations, the fighting was practically over. A total of 202 students were rescued in the town that day. After the fall of Pearl airport, Marines from the 22nd MAU launched a combined helicopter/Amtrac attack on an island 20 miles (32 km) north of Grenada. Their mission completed, by November 1 the Marines were back en route for their initial destination ... Beirut, and the paratroopers of the 82nd had returned to their base at Fort Bragg.

The American citizens had been airlifted safe and sound in the Starlifters.

11 American soldiers were killed in action and 116 American civil servants were injured. Grenadian casualties were 45 dead and 35 injured and Cuban casualties 35 dead and 59 injured.

The Panama assault: December 1989

In the morning of December 17, 1989, President George Bush Senior invited 50 old friends to spend Christmas Eve at the White House. The unexpected arrival during the evening of the "Joint Chiefs", the "Chairman", General Colin Powell, the Secretary of Defense, Richard Cheney and the National Security Advisor, Brent Snowcroft, meant "work comes first, as usual", but above all that there had just been a serious event.

On December 16, a Navy lieutenant on leave was killed by the troops of the Panama Defense Force (PDF). On the 18th, an army officer injured a corporal of the Panama police near American installations in the canal zone. Panama had been a headache for Washington for over a year. Drugs traffic from this region to the United States had escalated to enormous proportions. On May 9, a general election resulted in the victory of Manuel Antonio Noriega, generating considerable controversy due to allegations from the opposition led by Guillermo Endara, who claimed that the vote had been rigged.

George Bush was unable to keep his usual reserve any longer, Noriega was not going to stop there. The situation was going to deteriorate. Only one option was open to the United States: take action in Panama.

To take military control of the country, America had three objectives: 1) Contain the resistance of Noriega's forces; 2) Capture the dictator and bring him to the United States to stand trial on drugs trafficking charges (he had accumulated a considerable personal fortune through drugs); 3) Set up a stable government, led by Endara who declared that he had won the May elections.

The US already had 13,000 troops prepared for action, with armored vehicles and helicopters stationed on several bases in the Panama Canal zone. 2000 of these troops had been sent there as reinforcements at the start of 1989. The United States headquarters in the south was located just a few miles west of Panama City. The other neuralgic points included the PDF headquarters, also west of the city, the presidential "Palace", built on a promontory west of the Panama Bay, near Howard

Base, Allbrook station in the north, and Tocumen international airport, about 18 miles (30 km) east of the canal.

On December 20, 1989, 11,000 men were airlifted from the United States, ready for the landing. The 82nd Airborne Division was assigned to this operation and supplied an intervention brigade: the 3rd Brigade, comprising the 504th PIR and its support units, which would have to jump on Tocumen airport. The DZ would have been secured beforehand by a unit of Rangers.

As the 141 aircraft, carrying the 2nd Battalion of the 504th PIR flew over the DZ, located on the airport runways, enemy fire injured one paratrooper. Fifty other paratroopers were injured when landing.

The 1st Battalion of the 504th PIR jumped later, at 03h30. The last jump was carried out at 04h30, by men from the 325th.

There was never any doubt that the PDF (a mixture of soldiers and armed policemen) would put up no resistance. Washington's prime concern was that Noriega would escape into the jungle and organize Vietnam-style guerilla warfare, which could lad for years. In addition, George Bush, whose declared intention was to set up Endara's party in power, did not want public opinion to consider him as a puppeteer. He was also aware that there could be a reaction in Latin America against US involvement in Panama's political affairs.

Rangers and "All American" paratroopers were dropped over key positions and, to make sure there were no loopholes, a team of Navy Seals was dropped in the Panama Bay to attack the presidential palace and stop Noriega from escaping. At the very start of the attack, Guillermo Endara was sworn into the presidency by a Panama judge in the basements of an American military base.

At dawn, waves of air raids, armored vehicles and paratroopers were launched on Panama city while light tanks surrounded and set fire to the Comandancia, the PDF headquarters where Noriega's supporters fled for their lives. Two battalions took control of an electrical distribution center, Madden Dam and Renacer Prison in Gamboa. prison, where 48 former PDF members had been interned for staging a coup attempt to overthrow Noriega in October.

The air force carried out a successful sortie to neutralize the Panamanian troops at Fort Amador, west of the city, and airborne troops were dropped over a nearby runway to secure this region.

While the fighting to capture Noriega continued, the Americans, faced with little resistance, blocked off the bridge over river Pacora, which crosses Panama City, and sank PDF navy ships trying to escape. The outskirts of the city were in a state of chaos. The fiercest fighting had taken place around the Comandancia, the sound of machine gun fire there could be heard from the other side of Panama bay. Bombs and artillery fire rained down over the city without hitting any specific targets.

By December 20 in the afternoon, the 3rd Brigade had achieved all its objectives. The brigade had to remain in Panama, however, to restore order.

On January 6, the brigade was back at Fort Bragg.

Koweït

On August 2, 1990, Iraq decided to invade its neighbor Kuwait, causing an outcry from rest of the world. Oil seemed to be the main objective of this unexpected conflict. America could not remain indifferent to the attack on this small state and the risk of having one of its main suppliers of black gold in the Gulf, Saudi Arabia, invaded.

President George Bush Senior quickly took the decision to send the 82nd Airborne Division with a squadron of F-15 fighters, declaring that, "a line had been drawn in the sand".

In the evening of August 6, 1990, the telephone started to ring at Fort Bragg and in the Fayette-ville sector. The division was put on alert. At 07h00, the next morning, the division units sent in their preparation progress reports, first the 2nd Brigade (325th PIR), then the 3rd Brigade (505th PIR) and lastly the 1st Brigade (504th PIR). In addition to its infantry elements, each brigade comprised support, artillery, armored, engineering, medical corps, air defense, material, air support, intelligence, military police, chemical warfare and logistics units.

Special desert fighting equipment was issued to the men, desert camouflage uniforms, extra water bottles, new filter for M-17 gas masks, etc. At the same time, the division's vehicles were sent by ship from the ports of Wilmington and Norfolk, Virginia.

No-one really knew what the situation was in the Persian Gulf, especially regarding the strength of the Iraqi Army, massed along the border between Kuwait and Saudi Arabia. This explains why the 82nd had not received its mission orders before leaving Fort Bragg. They would have to improvise, depending on the events.

Fourteen hours after the alert, the first paratroopers boarded C-141 Starlifters at Pope AFB, destination Dhahran in Saudi Arabia. The first wave carried the 2nd Brigade. The division commander, Major General James H. Johnson, had decided not to accompany the 2nd Brigade but remain with the 3rd, ready to plan an airborne operation if the situation should deteriorate. The division's deputy commander, Brigadier General Richard Timmons, was ordered to accompany the 2nd Brigade. He commanded the division in the field until the rest of the division arrived.

The 82nd set up camp near Al-Jubayl, close to the Kuwaiti border. This was to become home for the 2nd Brigade until October 1. The other two brigades set up camp in the desert north west of Dharhan in a position called Champion Main. Whilst a strong American force started to build up in Saudi Arabia and the danger of an Iraqi attack dwindled, the 2nd Brigade was transferred near an airfield at Ab Qaiq, in anticipation of a large-scale operation. Over the next few months, the division took part in a training program designed to prepare the men for desert fighting.

On January 8, 1991, however, an Iraqi missile attack on the Saudi capital triggered the Quick Silver plan, aimed at protecting the strategic points in the town against any terrorist attack. American troops entered the capital.

The 505th PIR was transported to Riyadh until the start of the ground attack, on February 24, 1991.

Diplomatic channels failed to find a peaceful solution before the deadline imposed by President Bush for the withdrawal of Iraqi troops. Desert Shield was soon to become Desert Storm. The air phase which started on January 17, 1991 was to last one month. The air raids by the coalition squadrons inflicted devastating losses on the Iraqi troops. Everything of military value for the enemy was going to be destroyed.

For the ground offensive, the 82nd Division would liaise with the 6th French Armored Division and would have to drive deep into Iraq to protect the left flank of the Allies. The division was covertly moved near the Iraqi border on January 19. The 82nd would have to face the 45th Iraqi Infantry Division.

The 82nd was informed that it would have to launch its attack the day before the ground offensive, G-1. The 2nd Brigade would lead the attack with the 6th French Light Armored Division, followed by the 3rd Brigade (505th PIR) and the 1st Brigade (504th PIR).

By the time the ground attack started, the air offensive, after 37 days of non-stop attacks with 80,000 raids, had already reduced Iraqi forces by 50 percent. At this stage in the fighting, the allies had suffered only minimum casualties. On the other side of the border, the coalition force comprised 750,000 men ready for action.

At 11h00 on February 23, 1991, after 200 days spent in Saudi Arabia, the 2nd Brigade of the 82nd Division launched an assault on the mountainous positions of the enemy's 45th Infantry Division, which it found to be deserted. The French and the rest of the 82nd took this opportunity to thrust into Iraq. By the end of the day, the 82nd division with the French had penetrated 56 miles (90 km) into enemy territory. The division was submerged by the number of prisoners who had to be transferred to the rear and by the equipment left on the battlefield, which had to be destroyed. By the end of G+1, the Allies had captured over 20,000 enemy soldiers, the 82nd alone had captured over 1000. On February 26, the French left the 2nd Brigade which rejoined the division. The 2nd became the division's reserve brigade, while the 3rd and 1st Brigades headed north. Early the same day, contact had been made with the 101st Airborne Division "Screaming Eagles" 327th Infantry, operating on the right flank of the 82nd.

The next day (G+3), the division continued to attack along river Euphrates to cut off the enemy's line of retreat. The 82nd and the 101st with the 8th Corps had to prepare for transfer to Basra (Iraq's second largest city), where there was a risk of urban combat with the famous Iraqi Republican Guard. The objective of the 8th Corps was to wipe out this division and occupy Basra.

The attack proved unnecessary since on February 28, 1991 at 05h00, the paratroopers from the 82nd were informed of a cease-fire starting at 08h00.

The 82nd airborne suffered no casualties during this campaign.

On March 5, the division rejoined its positions in Saudi Arabia, before returning to Fort Bragg.

This was the first time since the Second World that the entire division had been sent into combat. Every soldier of the "All American" received the Combat Infantry Badge.

Irak

When America was attacked by terrorists on September 11, 2001, President George Bush Junior pledged to hunt down and destroy every terrorist nest throughout the world, especially the hideouts of the terrorist organization Al-Qaeda. Afghanistan was invaded, Iraq was to suffer the same fate.

In June 2002, the 82nd Airborne's Task Force Pan-

ther, comprised of elements from the 505th PIR and other 82nd units, deployed to Afghanistan in support of operation "Enduring Freedom". In January 2003, Task Force Devil, mainly comprised of the 504th PIR, replaced Task Force Panther and maintained the division's mission.

In February 2003, the 325th Airborne Infantry Regiment, Task Force Falcon, deployed in Kuwait to support the operation Iraqi Freedom. On January 19, 2004, the regiment was back at Fort Bragg. In September, the 505th and elements from the division's headquarters were deployed to Iraq for six months to relieve the 3rd Infantry Division. Like the 325th, their mission was to provide security for western Iraq.

The following photographic documentary on the War in Iraq contains no specific legends. The photographs were taken by a soldier during a tour in the Middle East. For security reasons, the locations and the names of the soldiers are not given.

We are at liberty to say, however, that the photographs recreate the route taken by Task Force Falcon comprising soldiers from the 325th Airborne Regiment of the 82nd Airborne Division from their arrival in Kuwait, where they were given special training in urban combat and combat techniques in Iraq, up to their baptism of fire in the major Iraqi cities.

1. Paratroopers from the 325th receive urban combat training in Saudi Arabia before leaving for Iraq. The weapons are equipped with a blank firing attachment.

2. The man standing up is about to fire his grenade launcher against the enemy position.

3. The NCO in the background is indicating the objectives, the man lying down is armed with an M-243.

4. In Saudi Arabia, the paratroopers from the 82nd receive special training in urban combat so that they are familiar with the techniques used by the enemy, before being transferred to Iraq.

5. While an NCO is observing a training exercise from the roof, the men infiltrate a village during a MOUT (Military Operation in Urban Terrain).

6. The first men to leave the house must take up a cover position.

7. In the meantime, the rest of the group exfiltrates the house.

8. Each man receives a firing angle, not forgetting the terraced roofs often used as firing positions by enemy snipers.

1

1. In Saudi Arabia, the paratroopers from the 325th receive special training (MOUT: Military Operation in Urban Terrain)

2 and **3.** This paratrooper is armed with an M-4 assault rifle.

4. The man on the ground is armed with a 5.56 light machine gun.

5, 6, 7, 8 and **9.** In Saudi Arabia, during the MOUT (Military Operation in Urban Terrain), paratroopers from the 325th learn how to get an injured soldier into cover before evacuation.

1. Paratroopers from the 325th preparing an M119 105 mm Howitzer for action.

2. On arrival in Saudi Arabia, the paratroopers from the 325th receive a briefing on combat techniques used by the Iraqis.

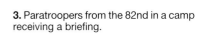

3. Paratroopers from the 82nd in a camp receiving a briefing.

4. Arsenal captured from the enemy, of Russian origin. In the foreground, two Mauser rifles.

5. Logistics has always been the strong point of the American army. On this photograph, the 82nd is receiving its weekly supplies flown in from the States.

6. While the guards are keeping a lookout from an observation post of the 82nd Airborne camp, rolls of barbed wire are waiting to be used to protect sensitive sectors.

4. Enemy forces are hiding in this village. After a burst of covering fire from the helicopters, the paratroopers are about to launch an attack on the village. Even though the men of the 82nd go into action quickly, some of the rebels manage to escape.

5. The section launches the assault, the man on the left is carrying a SMAW rocket launcher on his back.

1. Joint mission with the paratroopers from the 82nd and the helicopters whose role was to carry out surveillance and provide cover before the assault.

2. The paratroopers of the "All American" have taken up position along a road. On the other side in the palm grove, enemy soldiers are under artillery fire.

3. A section of paratroopers crossing the remains of an enemy unit destroyed by a bombing raid.

6. The section takes a minute's rest, the man in the foreground is armed with an M203 grenade launcher attached to an assault rifle and an M590 pump-action shotgun which he slipped on his backpack.

1. A section of paratroopers from the 82nd attacking a village. Blackhawk helicopters provide covering fire as well as air surveillance, in liaison with the ground troops.

2. On the ground, the men try to locate the enemy positions before infiltrating the village.

3. The men from the section are in position and have dropped their backpacks, ready to launch the assault. M-240 and M-249 light machine guns will cover the GIs as they advance.

4. The men have taken up position on the outskirts of the village in a rubbish tip.

5. Two paratroopers from the 325th observe an enemy position from the shelter of a railroad line.

1. A section of the 325th advancing along a road under the protection of .50-caliber machine guns atop Humvees.

2. A section has just discovered an isolated enemy shooter; he will be suppressed by a soldier from the 325th armed with an M-40 sniper rifle with scope.

3. A section advancing along a wall in a village.

4. A GI armed with an M-4 is ammunition bearer for the M-240 machine gun and carries a rocket on his back.

5. This photograph shows the special gear worn by GIs in Iraq: Kevlar helmet, bulletproof vest, gas mask, tube of the water bottle carried on the back, knee pads and plastic ties carried around the belt to attach prisoners.

1. Men from the 82nd advancing in an oil refinery.

2. A paratrooper from the 82nd armed with an M-240 machine gun has taken up position opposite some warehouses; the rest of the unit is advancing under cover.

3. A paratrooper armed with an M-4 and a smoke grenade has taken up position in a destroyed public building. Every moment of respite must be taken under cover.

4. A machine gunner from the 82nd on the turret of his Humvee is observing the sector through the telescope of his .50-caliber machine gun.

5. At sunset, a .50-caliber gunner from the "All American" observing the sector from his Humvee; everything seems calm.

1. This paratrooper from the 325th armed with an M-4 is carrying a SMAW rocket launcher.

2. A paratrooper from the 82nd Airborne is armed with an M-249 Squad Automatic Weapon (SAW).

3. A section of the 82nd is advancing in a village, the man at the front is armed with an M-249 with telescopic sight.

4. A paratrooper from the 82nd entering a house, armed with an M590 Riot Gun.

5. Protected by a truck, a GI is observing the desert.

1. A section of Humvees stopped in the desert.

2. A convoy of Humvees from the 325th has just joined a main road leading to Baghdad. While the men are taking up position along the road, the vehicles move to different firing angles to cover the entire fire zone.

3. On arrival in the major towns, the paratroopers from the 82nd are enthusiastically welcomed by opponents of Saddam Hussein's regime.

4. The Americans issue food and water to the isolated populations which stopped receiving supplies at the start of the war.

5. On the roads, some civilians welcome the liberators with a certain degree of skepticism.

6. While others demonstrate their happiness as the troops who overthrew Saddam Hussein arrive.

1. A section advancing in a village occupied by the enemy. This interesting photograph shows the number of different weapons used by an airborne section.

2. A section advancing in a village, the man in the front is armed with a LAW (Light Antitank Weapon) rocket launcher.

3. A light section of the 325th advancing in the village, the man on the left has a camera, his film will be used to provide news coverage of the division.

4. Paratroopers from a reconnaissance section advancing in a narrow alley in the village. The enemy is everywhere and ready to make the supreme sacrifice to exterminate the "Infidels".

1. Two paratroopers from the 325th enter a village and start to search every house. They are armed with the M-4 assault rifle, successor of the M-16.

2. A team from the 325th advancing in the village, the man in the front is armed with an M-240 machine gun, the second with an M-4 equipped with a grenade launcher.

3. An M-249 machine gunner covers the rear of a section advancing in a village.

4. The enemy has been localized, the attack must be carried out from the rear to surprise them and prevent escape.

5. Like their predecessors in the Second World War, the paratroopers of the 82nd use a phrase book to communicate with the local populations.

1. A team o f the 325th armed with M-4s, observes a village from a copse of trees. The man at the front is the radio operator, the second carrying binoculars is an NCO and the third is responsible for protecting the team.

2. On open terrain, such as desert areas, soldiers in a section can take cover behind the slightest fold in the ground or obstacle as they advance.

3. Two paratroopers from the All American, along the Baghdad-Hilla railroad line.

4. A Humvee stopped in front of a portrait of Saddam Hussein painted on a wall.

1. This paratrooper, armed with an M-4 assault rifle, is standing guard during a food handout to Iraqi civilians.

2. A paratrooper from the 325th is inspecting the underneath of a vehicle entering a secured zone.

3. A section of the 325th makes contact with Iraqi civilians to discover the enemy hideouts. The populations in favor of the coalition must be reassured and treated with consideration.

4. A suspicious house is about to be searched. Before entering, the men must install a penetration device.

5. Exhausted paratroopers from the 82nd take a short break under the friendly eyes of Iraqi children.

6. As in every war, children are attracted by the soldiers and are waiting for the GIs to give them candies.

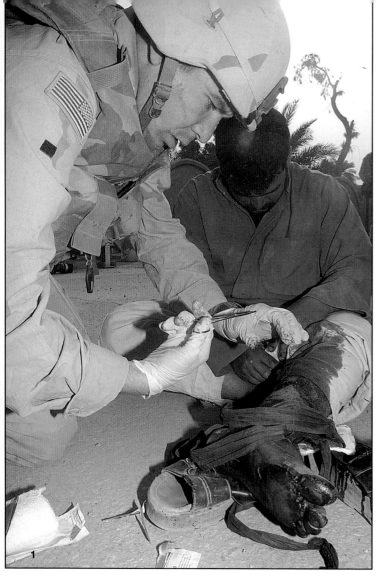

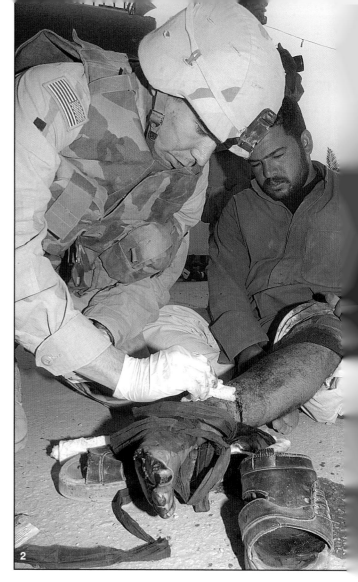

1, 2 and 3. A medic from the 325th is giving first aid to an injured prisoner. Management of the numerous Iraqi injured and prisoners is a critical problem for the allied forces.

4, 5 and 6. Emergency MEDEVAC. Rotation of UH-60 Blackhawk belonging to a medical unit. They are bringing back injured from Baghdad. From the helicopter, the injured are transported in an M113 ambulance to the first aid station at brigade headquarters.

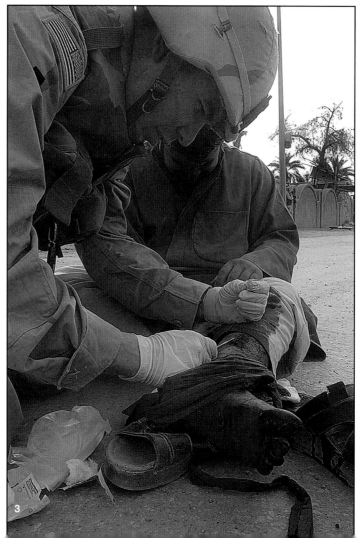

Achevé d'imprimer le 25 mai 2006
sur les presses de
Ferre Olsina S.A.
Barcelone, Espagne
pour le compte des Editions Heimdal